Surviving the Fire

"One who forgets the last war
prepares for the next one."

Dorothee Sölle

SURVIVING THE FIRE

MOTHER COURAGE
& WORLD WAR II

EDITED BY LILO KLUG

OPEN HAND

OPEN HAND PUBLISHING INC.
Seattle, Washington

Open Hand Publishing Inc.
P.O. Box 22048
Seattle, WA 98122
(206) 323-3868

Cover illustration by Ulrike Schuck-Evezard
Cover design by Deb Figen

FIRST EDITION

Library of Congress Cataloging-in-Publication Data

Heimatfront. English.
    Surving the fire: Mother Courage & World War II / edited by Lilo Klug.
        p.   cm.
    Translation of: Heimatfront.
    Produced by the Werkstattgruppe der Frauen Für Frieden/Heilbronn.
    ISBN 0-940880-23-7 : $17.95. — ISBN 0-940880-24-5 (pbk.): $9.95
        1. World War, 1939-1945 — Women — Germany. 2. World War, 1939-1945 — Personal narratives, German. 3. Germany — History — 1933-1945.
I. Klug, Kilo, 1933-   . II. Werkstattgruppe der Frauen
für Frieden/Heilbronn (Germany) III. Title.
D810.W7W4713   1989
940.53' 15042' 0943 — dc20   89-22926
                                                    CIP

Printed in the United States of America

TABLE OF CONTENTS

GERMANY 1939

CHRONOLOGY OF THE SECOND WORLD WAR

Jan. 30, 1933	Adolf Hitler becomes chancellor of Germany
Oct. 14, 1933	Germany leaves League of Nations
Mar. 1936	Germany remilitarizes the Rhineland
Mar. 13, 1938	Germany annexes Austria
Sept. 30, 1938	Munich conference approves German acquisition of Sudetenland in Czechoslovakia
Mar. 15, 1939	Germany occupies rest of Czechoslovakia
Sept. 1, 1939	Germany invades Poland, official start of WW II
Apr. 9, 1940	Germany invades Norway and Denmark
May 10, 1940	Beginning of German invasion of Low Countries and France
July 10, 1940	Germany begins air assault on Britain
June 22, 1941	Germany invades U.S.S.R.
Dec. 5, 1941	German offensive stalls 25 miles from Moscow
Jan. 16, 1943	Berlin is raided by British Royal Air Force (RAF) for first time since Nov. 7, 1941.
June 22, 1943	U.S. Eighth Air Force makes first large scale daylight raid on Ruhr area of Germany
Oct. 14, 1943	U.S. Eighth Air Force raids Schweinfurt ball-bearing plants
Feb. 13, 1944	Allies fire-bomb Dresden
Mar. 4, 1944	First U.S. air raid on Berlin
May 12, 1944	U.S. Eighth Air Force attacks oil plants in central Germany
June 6, 1944	Allies land in France (D-Day)
July 20, 1944	German assassination attempt on Hitler fails
Aug. 25, 1944	Allies occupy Paris
Dec. 4, 1944	Allies fire-bomb Heilbronn
Jan. 1, 1945	Last major German air raid made on Allies airfield
Jan. 17, 1945	Russia captures Poland
Apr. 7, 1945	Russia enters Vienna
Apr. 30, 1945	U.S. Seventh Army occupies Munich
Apr. 30, 1945	Hitler commits suicide
May 7, 1945	German High Command surrenders all forces unconditionally, at Reims
May 9, 1945	European hostilities officially end

ACKNOWLEDGMENTS

Many people participated in the making of this book; first of all the women who relived and wrote down the painful stories from their war experience. The original idea for the book was that of Christl Banghard-Jost whose patience and understanding enabled the women to overcome the difficulties they had in recalling the war years, then writing about them.

Special thanks, of course, to the translators: first of all to Hilda Freyd, who did a tremendous job, and also to Bettina Lande, Ruth Turner, Janet Miller-Goeder, Elizabeth Lempp, Larry Swingle, Carol Bornhauser and Elizabeth Gannon. Without their help the English edition of this book would not have been possible.

There are other people whose support and advice we appreciate very much. Finally, I want to express my gratitude to Phyllis Hatfield, the editor of this English-language edition, and to Anna Rodieck of Open Hand Publishing who made it possible to have the book published in the United States and who gave it its final shape.

INTRODUCTION

Heilbronn is a medium-sized town with approximately 110,000 inhabitants. It is situated in West Germany between sloping vineyards and forested hills in the Neckar Valley, an extensive, densely populated, industrialized area.

In Heilbronn, as well as in other towns in Germany, there is a "Women for Peace" group. This group considers itself to be a part of the worldwide peace movement. Its work for peace wasn't any different from that of other groups until one day in 1975 in a nearby recreational area — an idyllic spot where the people of Heilbronn often went for their Sunday walks — a large tract of land was secured with many rows of barbed wire, floodlights and watchtowers. Frogs, salamanders, cotton-grass and nightingales disappeared, and the inhabitants of the town were no longer allowed to set foot on their beloved *Waldheide*, as the area is called.

When worried citizens asked questions, they were told that a training ground for U.S. soldiers was being built. It soon became apparent, however, that by no means was this to be a harmless training ground. Rather, it was to be a base for the installation of Pershing missiles.

Although members of the peace groups were deeply shocked, the majority of the people of Heilbronn took little notice of what was happening under their very noses. The Women for Peace asked themselves, "Where are the people who lived during the Second World War? They should be the very first to protest against this new missile base. Didn't they vow in 1945 that never again would war issue forth from German soil? Where are all of the people who took that vow? Surely they must have taken it in earnest."

We decided to look into the matter. And thus began the idea of writing this book. The women of the war generation would have their say. They, like women in all wars, suffered silently and made sacrifices. They weren't asked, they were ordered.

The women who wanted to work on this book met together. Adopting the name "Workshop Group," they wrote articles for the local newspaper and invited women of the war generation to work with them. Initially about fifteen women came forward. When the word got around, there were soon over thirty of us. Each woman wrote down her story or, if she didn't want to write, recorded her experiences on a tape cassette. Most of us had never written or published anything before. We met every second week to read our stories aloud and to discuss them.

Those women who had experienced the war were now between forty-five and eighty-five years old. Through the meetings and the discussions each one grew more devoted to this work. The feeling of being able to do something meaningful, to pass on one's life experiences, was wonderful.

Through this new activity new contacts were made and new interests sprang up. Understanding and communication between the generations improved with each meeting.

In the beginning many of us found it difficult to dig out the old, painful stories. We shrank back from our memories, but then, encouraged by the example of others, we tackled the task. It often hurt to tear open the old wounds. Many times, when the memories were too overwhelming, words simply failed us. Gradually we discovered that after writing and speaking about the experiences of the war we came away from the meetings less encumbered. Many of us realized only then how difficult it still is to carry around with us the dregs of that period of our lives.

Unfortunately, despite all our efforts, we weren't able to find participants who had been active in a Nazi organization — BDM-*Bund Deutscher Mädchen* (League of German Girls), NS-*Frauenschaft* (Nazi Women's Union) or NSDAP-*National Sozialistische Arbeiter Partei* (the Nazi Party). Women who were abused, and Jewish women are also not represented. They certainly could have brought forth aspects which would have been valuable in rounding out the picture of this era. On the other hand, many of the Workshop women belonged to resistance groups during the Nazi rule and are today, as far as their strength allows, in the peace movement.

Surviving The Fire isn't meant to be a historical reference book. We have told our stories subjectively, filtered only through our own memories. We haven't tried through hindsight to readjust the events historically. We are speaking about people and about women's sufferings during wartime, whether in Heilbronn or elsewhere.

To return to the question asked at the beginning, "Why aren't the people of the war generation more active in the peace movement?"

We, the Workshop women, can answer this question in so far as it pertains to us. I believe that most of us are simply afraid of the problems. We want to have our peace and quiet; we don't want to hear anything more about war and armament. We still feel as if we are victims of history and we haven't accepted that it is not only those who commit a crime that are guilty, but also those who allow the crime to occur.

And there is something else. Those difficult years didn't pass by without leaving their mark. Many of the people of the war generation became sick and have suffered from sleeplessness for many years. Their strength has been sapped by their struggle to survive beyond the agony and the mourning for those who died. Many are very tired. They cannot deal with today's problems because they no longer have the necessary energy. We have written our book for these women as well.

Meanwhile the populace of Heilbronn has been awakened. On January 11, 1985, a tragic accident occurred in which a Pershing II missile caught fire, killing three soldiers and wounding sixteen others. This accident proved to people that we are living on a powder keg, that the threat of war doesn't just exist in the heads of a few pacifists, but is a reality.

On February 4, 1985, 10,000 people walked, in the pouring rain, to the Pershing missile site to protest against the missiles. In addition, the Heilbronn City Council has unanimously declared the missiles to be undesirable. Today we know that the majority of the inhabitants of Heilbronn are behind us in our efforts to bring about a more peaceful world. We know that it is more important than ever to remember and not to forget.

For that reason we are addressing our stories especially to those who will come after us, those who luckily have never experienced war, but who, despite this, should never forget what war is.

We chose the subtitle "Mother Courage and World War II." Mother Courage has been a symbol for women in war ever since the seventeenth century, when the German writer J.J.C. von Grimmelshausen first wrote about her in his book about the Thirty Years War, *Simplicius Simplicissimus*. Bertold Brecht dedicated his famous play *Mother Courage* to her. Mother Courage stands for women in war throughout European history. Women who lost their fathers, their husbands, their sons and their homes; women who were not interested in either victory or power, but whose only concern was to survive and to be able to protect and to feed their children.

We hope that this book will be taken as a warning and as a summons to be alert, to be critical, to be troublesome and to say no at the right moment, so that what we tell here will never happen again.

Lilo Klug, 1989

3

THE BUILDUP &
EARLY WAR YEARS

Born 1912. Worked with the underground resistance during the Nazi era and as an office worker after the war. Retired since 1975. Has one daughter and eight grandchildren.

1942

We Watched the Gestapo Outside

I was born in the year 1912, in Heilbronn, a provincial town nestled in the hills above the Neckar River. I wasn't quite four when I started going to kindergarten. The governesses in their white starched caps, richly pleated grey uniforms and stiff white collars filled me with awe.

This was during the time of the First World War and my mother was constantly at home, sitting in front of the sewing machine. The room was filled with baskets brimming over with uniform braiding, jackets, thread and other sewing implements, shiny buttons, leather buttons and empty spools. I enjoyed playing with the spools and buttons while singing the school songs of the day,

such as "Hail to Thee, Victory's Wreath," or songs about enemies —
"The French Soldiers Who Wore Red Trousers" or the one about the
enemy who "walked about in fur, with shaggy hair and even ate
candles" [a reference to the Russians].

Since my father had been assigned to a communications unit,
he often came home for a few days at a time. My mother felt awkward in front of the other women in the house whose husbands were
at the front and were therefore the heroes we were praying for at
school.

I gathered from the discussions at home — more from feeling
than anything else — that my father didn't care at all about being a
hero. Neither did he view the French as enemies, but rather as men
who also had wives and children at home. Every now and then he
went to the countryside to hoard flour, lard and eggs that he later
brought home.

I was aware that the war was over when I noticed the marvel-
ous, tasty cream toffees in my Aunt Marie's store and Aunt Marie
commented that they were peace bonbons and, thank God, the terrible war was over. In the meantime it had also dawned on me that
war was something bad, that it only brought misfortune and that
many people had to die senselessly. Several of my girlfriends in the
neighborhood were wearing black bows in their pigtails because
their fathers had died in action. Their mothers' eyes were often red
from crying. It hurt, deep inside my childish heart.

As it turned out, when I began to go to elementary school,
many of the older teachers still defended Germany's aggression in
the First World War. My parents' friends, however, were mostly
democrats and socialist-minded. During their conversations in the
living room I often picked up much that would be beneficial and
valuable in my later life. One sentence especially, I heard frequently.
It was written on the very first page of a green book my father had:
"First we are all human beings, after that Europeans, and only then
are we Germans."

There was a monist, a syndicalist and an anarchist in our neighborhood. There were freethinkers, those who were nudist enthusi-
asts, plus disciples of this or that movement. They were all invited to
our place. My mother fed them, while my father wanted to send
them to the fields to harvest potatoes, an idea which they rejected,
living as they were in the intellectual realm.

The number of conservatives and German nationalists calling
for discipline and for law and order in dealing with the rebellious
Left increased. They glorified military life and war. At a school-
mate's house I looked at great big books about soldiers, victorious
heroes with their flags, dying heroes who were German victors. His

sister played the national anthem on the piano, although she played quite softly. If her father came in, he invariably praised her. I mentioned none of this at home. My instinct kept me from it, since my father didn't like such military types.

Much has been written about the struggle of those who opposed the war. They splintered into too many parties and organizations, and only at the end of the 1920s was the great danger of Nazism recognized. By then it was too late.

Once during this time I was invited, along with other young socialists, to the home of a Jewish family. The conversation got interesting as we debated and politicized. I have never forgotten how one young social democrat, when asked about the Nazi danger, replied, "Oh, there are only a few of those swastika types!" Although I didn't understand very much about politics at that time, I considered that a dangerous attitude. I was greatly relieved when several months later this particular Jewish family succeeded in escaping abroad.

The Nazis took control in 1933. I was standing on an avenue together with some other young people, hedged in among the crowd. Everything — the newspaper, the labor unions, the public offices — had been taken over by the SA [*Sturmabteilung* — stormtroopers], by those "noble old fighters." Victory was announced over the loudspeakers. "Everything is under the command of the Führer! Hail! Hail! Hail!" There was hysteria on all sides. But those standing around us were motionless and silent.

Those people with leftist views — somehow the Hitlerites knew who they were — were taken into "protective custody" a few days later and transported to Heuberg [a concentration camp]. Others were locked in prisons. Those who dared to defend themselves were taken to the "Brown House" [the local Nazi party headquarters], where they were beaten up by the Nazis. Despite all this, isolated fliers still turned up. Slogans calling for resistance still appeared on fences each morning. Finally, as more people were arrested, scarcely any resistance fighters remained at large.

Hatred toward Jews was fomented in everyday life, and Jewish shops were boycotted. I knew many Jewish families from my schooldays. I learned again and again with relief that this or that family had fled abroad. The life of those remaining was a tragedy; hardly anyone of them survived.

In 1934 a Heilbronn communist and resistance fighter, Gottlob Feidengruber, managed to escape from his cell and flee with his wife, Rose, to the Saar district which was at that time under French control. I knew both of them very well, so when Rose wrote to me regarding the shipment of a few pieces of clothing, I sent off a package to the address given and wrote Gottlob a letter as well.

We also attempted to flee to the Saar district. At least, through Gottlob, we had a base there. Day by day, surveillance on us was increasing. We used to meet by arrangement in the apartment of a friend of my mother's, an opponent of the Nazis. Most of our friends had already been placed under detention. We would deliberate on how best to distribute fliers or paint large-lettered slogans on conspicuous places. As we talked we could look out of the window and see one or two Gestapo officers constantly pacing to and fro on the other side of the street.

During one of our get-togethers a member of our group, extremely upset, arrived and said: "The Gestapo is right behind me. They've been following me for days. I can't land in their clutches again. They recently gave me a bad beating in the Brown House." He looked toward the kitchen window at the tall pear tree standing outside and said, "I can climb down and beat it over the tracks." Shortly thereafter the doorbell rang. In an instant Fritz was on the kitchen table and then out on a high branch of the tree. We closed the window and two other men in our group vanished down the staircase into a lavatory which had been built on the side of the building, as was common in such old houses.

Two of the Gestapo, who knew us by name, came into the kitchen, looked at us two women and went into the other rooms. "So then, where are our painters?" A short verbal skirmish. The younger of the two officers was a big cynic, a really nasty guy. "Oh, Fred," I answered. "He had a bad case of diarrhea." "Well, where is that quiet little place [a colloquialism for the lavatory]?" They went and checked it out then said, "Well, indeed it is quiet. No one's there, but it doesn't matter. A few days aren't so important to us."

Fritz's fast descent had saved him for the time being. He prepared to escape to the Saar district and within a few days set off on his bicycle early in the evening. I accompanied him as far as Neckarsulm. Addresses and such had to be memorized.

On November 8, 1934, at seven in the morning, I was arrested in my apartment. Two Gestapo officers took me to the local prison. As I was going through the courtyard, I heard a familiar whistle, a signal which told me that one of our group had been caught at the border and was being held in detention. He had already spent time in "protective custody" and had also been wanting to go to the Saar. The whistle clued me in and I prepared myself accordingly.

We remained in detention in Heilbronn until March 1935. All the cells in both the district and regional courts were filled with Nazi opponents — communists, members of the Communist Youth, social democrats, foes of the regime with no party affiliation, Bible scholars, people of conscience.

I was granted an amnesty in March 1935, when the Saar district was handed over to Germany. My friend, however, was taken to the prison in Ulm, from which he escaped several months later. Through a daring flight and hitchhiking in a truck, he landed in Stuttgart, where he managed to hide himself for a short while in a summer house. But then he was arrested again, tried in Stuttgart and sentenced to one year in prison in Heilbronn. That came as a relief to him. Prison was, at least, humane. The concentration camps were hell. After that year, though, he did end up in a concentration camp. He was sent to Weltzheim, where the guards, uneducated fellows from the lowest social strata, set their huge dogs on people who were opposed to the murderous regime. Time and again terrible crimes are committed in the name of blind nationalism.

During the time I was in detention, first in one jail and then in another, my mother endeavored to have me released. She collected signatures and talked with Nazi functionaries trying to persuade them of my innocence. At the time, I was twenty-one. My four-year-old child was with my parents.

One day, as I was getting my hair cut in the corridor of the jail, the hairdresser mentioned that according to the newspaper, I had been arrested on charges of attempted treason, which, he thought, carried the death penalty. He only wanted to warn me, since it seemed that I had no idea how serious my situation really was.

I remained calm, not letting the guards notice anything. They themselves weren't exactly happy with the new regime, either, and treated us prisoners humanely. At least I never heard or experienced anything to the contrary — as far as the guards in Heilbronn were concerned. One said to me once, "Young girl, life isn't treating me any better than you. After all, I am spending my entire days, weeks and months in prison too."

I should mention also the court counselor who had to interrogate me every other day. I could detect that he was decent by nature. Certainly he was no Nazi. But I made it difficult for him to help me, since I was young, a vehement foe of fascism, war and inhumanity, and suffered with those who were suffering — a countless number at that time. Finally I was released upon certain conditions — where I could and could not work, and so on.

I recognized more and more the fact that whoever had eyes in their head and a modicum of clear, common sense, had to have realized that the mental control of the masses, the incitement against the Jews and dissidents, and the glorification of the "master race" would lead to war.

My father, during this period, was forcibly dispossessed of a piece of property which had been in the family for generations. He was threatened with the concentration camp when, full of indignation, he dropped by to see the district leader. Soon thereafter the Ludendorff barracks were built on his property.

Sometime in July 1939, I was taking my usual walk in the woods. From under the tall trees on the edge of the woods I looked down upon the town, whose every street and alleyway I knew. The trees all around looked like green billows against the blue sky — what a magnificent world had been bestowed on us! And who were those in power over us? Megalomaniacs, brutes!

Standing on the edge of the woods I saw a vision — silver birds crisscrossing the sky, bombs falling to the earth. I embraced a nearby tree, standing there and knowing that it would happen just like that. The war began shortly afterwards. Ruthlessly, without warning, other nations were attacked by Germany — Poland, Czechoslovakia, Russia, France — houses were burned, fields destroyed, people murdered — children, mothers, the old. As genocide and mass murder took place, announcements of victory boomed from the loudspeakers. The fascists celebrated their greatest triumphs, for "today Germany belongs to us, and tomorrow the entire world."

War was raging in other countries. Oh, how good that was to my fellow Germans! We had apartments, work, enough to eat. There were a great many celebrations held by Nazi families. "Of what concern are the others to us? The mass murders and executions, the concentration camps? That's all lies."

People like me were reserved and cautious. The greatest asset at the time was having two or three people whom one could trust. I was provided with such wealth during the entire Nazi period, and that gave me strength.

Meanwhile, the bombs were falling every now and then on the town — dropped by solo pilots, the so-called "Charlie bombers." There were the first civilian fatalities, the first houses destroyed.

It became quite dangerous for me once when I was attending a Nazi family celebration. An announcement of victory was once again blaring from the radio. "Our boys have succeeded in sinking a British ship with the entire crew." Then music, raptures of joy, "for we're heading, for we're heading, we're heading now for England." I was unable to join in the joyous ecstasy surrounding me. I happened to mention that at that precise moment there were many grieving mothers and wives in England. I felt the glance of the mistress of the house, fearless and loyal, and then: "I don't want to hear such a thing in our home. You'd better watch out, and your father, too, or else they'll [the authorities] have to do something." From then on I avoided those people and their apartment as much as possible.

Born 1919. Worked during the war as a forced laborer in the arms industry. Lost several members of her family in air raids. Married 1943. Has one daughter and two granddaughters.

1943

1985

Compulsory Wartime Service

The year was 1940 and I had been working for six years at a firm in Heilbronn when one day I was called into the manager's office. A few young girls were already in the office, and an officer of the SA [*Sturmabteilung* — Stormtroopers] and two ladies were sitting at the desk. "Heil Hitler" was the greeting. We stood there, full of anxiety. What did this mean? Had we perhaps said something we should not have? One could never be sure. We were given a brief explanation: "With the men at the front, there is a lack of workers everywhere. Therefore you women will have to take their places. This is compulsory wartime service. You are to report to work in Neckarsulm at the NSU. Be there one week from today, no later than seven a.m.! Heil Hitler." Just like that. No explanation of what the NSU works was. I thought it was where motorbikes and bicycles were manufactured.

Exactly one week later, more than fifty young women were standing at the main gate of NSU. We were let inside and our names were read out. The head of the factory, dressed in a SA uniform, made a speech. He spoke of our doing our duty at home, of being proud to be allowed to help win the great victory for our Fatherland. This was followed by "Sieg Heil, Sieg Heil, Sieg Heil!" Following that we were sent to our appointed work stations and ordered not to speak to any foreigners. Then prisoners of war were escorted in and kept under the constant surveillance of a German guard. From their clothes we could determine where they came from — Poland, France, even some from Russia. It was so strange. We young women exchanged many a questioning look at one another.

I very soon learned what the term "compulsory service" meant. This was indeed the beginning of an unhappy period in my life. Nobody was concerned about how we got to the factory or how we got home late at night. I went back and forth on my bike. I left Heilbronn at five each morning and returned at ten at night.

My new work was in a huge, noisy room where metal was stamped and perforated by gigantic machines. I was led to one of the machines and the foreman said: "There, here we are. You are to work here, young lady. Duty for your Fatherland." I had imagined that I would be assembling bicycles, and was terrified by these huge machines. This was work for a strong man. The foreman must have seen the fright on my face, for he said: "Your dainty hands are probably too fine for this." Nevertheless I had to learn to operate the machine. It was hard work and required a great deal of energy. My job was to perforate holes in iron parts which were laid in oil. Later I found out that these were parts for tanks.

I wondered what my future would be like. How would I endure the coarse behavior of the bosses and the guards? Where oh where had I landed? I was very unhappy. And to serve my Fatherland!

My hands had become so sore that I could hardly touch the handlebars of my bike. The seriousness of the war became increasingly apparent. There were more and more air-raid alerts, and often I had to cycle to work amidst falling bombs. Frequently after working my shift I sat for hours in a ditch at the side of the street, trembling with fear.

The oily metal damaged my hands to the point that my fingers would often bleed. My letters asking to be transferred to another job were refused with the remark: "You have to behave like a man!" A

Frenchman who worked near me and whose job it was to count small machine parts all day, would often look with pity in my direction. A slight nod of his head, an encouraging smile, offered some comfort.

At last I was transferred to another department, where my job was to cut and bore metal. My hands did not heal. I was still standing at a machine for long hours helping to produce parts for tanks to be used in the war. I could not and I would not continue!

Being sent home for a few days marked the end of a very difficult period in my young life. The doctor who treated me applied for my release from compulsory war service. I was thus able to return to work in my old firm, where I remained until it was completely destroyed during an air raid on December 4, 1944.

Born 1921. Worked during the war in an air force communications unit in France and in eastern Germany. Married. Has one daughter and two grandchildren.

1943

Nobody Gave Us a Ride

*I*n 1940, like all young unmarried women, I was put on active wartime duty, in Neckarsulm, not far from Heilbronn, where I grew up. I was on control duty in a secret armament factory where parts for munitions were manufactured. The strong smell of oil so affected my health that I was given six months' sick leave. That was really something unusual in the Third Reich!

Afterwards I reported for duty at the district war office, which sent me to a barracks at Augsburg. There I noticed how many of the young women were from Heilbronn. Many of us had no job and the military offered some opportunity for employment.

We learned the difference between all types of planes — foreign and German. We were expected to know the abbreviations and meanings of codes which were transmitted by telephone. Sometimes we were obliged to exercise in the barracks yard, but we were not trained to shoot.

After completing a nine-month training period at Christmas, we were allowed to choose where we wanted to go — Poland, Greece, or France. I chose France, although I couldn't speak any French. None of us had ever been so far away from home before and we were all looking forward to the journey. Once in Bordeaux, France, some members of our group were sent for duty in offices, the post office, or cloakrooms. We were not allowed to work in the kitchen; only men worked there.

I was sent to work in the central telegraph office because my hearing was good and I could write very quickly. Furthermore, I could sketch and design well. We received reports of the movements of enemy planes, and I sketched these on a card so that their course could be observed and followed.

It was very quiet and peaceful in Bordeaux until the invasion came. I was on duty that night and I was not able to leave the telephone for even a second. One troop-ship after the other was reported. It was the hardest night I have ever experienced. From that moment on, our free time was reduced, we had to be at home at eight o'clock and we had to get a permit for everything we did. Not long after that the women were ordered back home to Germany.

It was in Bordeaux that I met my future husband. Because we did not want to be separated, I delayed my journey back to Germany for as long as I possibly could. Finally, all the army women helpers and many civilians, as well as all able-bodied men fit for the front, were sent back to Germany in what was said to be the "last train." The entire train was occupied by members of the German Wehrmacht [armed forces]. We were waiting for an exceedingly long time at the Bordeaux train station and we wondered why the train didn't start. Then we learned that there had been an air-raid alert. But when the train finally started, it was headed in the wrong direction! We wanted to go south to Toulouse, but instead we were going north. The train stopped at an unknown station where we stayed all night. The next day we returned to Bordeaux again, where we stayed without any food. Somebody told us that the train could not proceed because the track to Toulouse had been destroyed by Partisans. Finally we left Bordeaux by truck, driving through a region infested with Partisans who often shot at us.

We did manage to arrive safely in Toulouse. There were crowds of soldiers and civilians filling the station, all trying to get back to Germany. The whole retreating army was jammed together, because the tracks had been destroyed. Once again we had to try to proceed by truck. Very often the soldiers were not willing to take us with them because in a critical situation we might become a hindrance — we could not shoot, we could not drive. And it was very dangerous; we were being followed and attacked by British bombers. We traveled mostly by night and stayed in villages or towns during the day, because civilians as a rule were not attacked.

Most of the French people had left their homes and were staying in the nearby woods. We fed ourselves on black bread and grapes which we picked from the vines. Sometimes our soldiers caught and killed a few chickens. That provided us with a good meal. Everything we needed had to be found in the farmyards. When the soldiers were looking for sleeping quarters, they simply broke the windows of empty houses and climbed in. We women, too, often slept in empty houses. I reflect today on how very dangerous it was. If the French who lived there came back during the night, they might have killed us.

Once English fighters came flying very low, but we were able to reach a French village before they saw us. We stayed there, huddled up in the empty houses, for about two hours. When we left our hiding place we saw that the trucks which had brought us had disappeared. We had to go and look for them. We found them all — completely burned out! A German train also stood in flames on the railway track.

We walked to the French town of Nîmes, where we looked for something to eat. Nîmes was crowded with German soldiers and civilians, and we all wanted to get back to Germany as quickly as possible, but there were no more trains.

We stood on the roadside three days and three nights waiting for a truck to give us a lift. One German officer's car after another passed us by without stopping. We felt miserable and forsaken. Worst of all, in almost every car there was a French girl! We felt cheated, because we had been put into a train which the officers knew would never arrive in Germany, while they drove automobiles back home that would arrive quickly.

Small horse-carts like the ones which had been used in the Russian campaign were being used for the retreat. Tanks and trucks were stuffed full with soldiers and civilians. Soldiers were hanging onto the footboards. Once when a truck slid into a ditch and struck a stone wall before coming to a halt, the flesh was torn away from the bone of a young officer's arm. The pain was so intense that the young man almost fainted. Soldiers hoisted the truck out of the ditch, and I was told to bandage the officer's arm. I had to muster all my strength to do that. The man developed fever and I was told to watch over and care for him. The soldiers said that since I was a woman, I had stronger nerves than they. We did not know where to find an ambulance. There was none to be found anywhere.

During the daytime we camped in the woods and I saw to it that my patient got plenty of tea to drink. One evening the soldiers became very nervous, and they finally told us that they had been given an ultimatum to surrender — we were surrounded by Partisans. After deliberation, the soldiers decided to go to the nearest village and place every truck that could be found into a long line. Armed with hand grenades and machine guns they awaited an attack. Another young woman, myself, and the gravely wounded officer were to lie down in a ditch and wait silently. Nobody knew what the outcome would be, and the suspense was awful. In the end, the Partisans did not attack. Towards daybreak we moved on. We received a radio message that there was an ambulance in the woods nearby and that our patient was to be brought there. I had to accompany the wounded officer alone into the woods. Once there, it took a long time before I was finally able to locate the camouflaged ambulance.

We were still on the retreat, near Dijon, when the American troops arrived in Paris. We were fired at heavily by the American bombers, which followed our retreat. At one point we had just entered the confines of a small French town when a bomb exploded. There was an indescribably loud explosion and shortly afterwards a German soldier came riding toward us on a bike and informed us that a direct hit had destroyed the railway bridge, leaving six people dead and thirty severely injured. That was war in all its horror.

Leaving the town, we were driving through dense woods in which Partisans were hiding when we were caught in a cloudburst. The rain was so intense that it started a landslide. Also, the motor in our truck became flooded and the driver could not get it started again. Finally we ended up having to push the truck into the next village. Rainwater flooded down the streets of the village. Looking closely, I saw that the water had a reddish tint. A soldier who had ridden on before to find quarters for us explained that there had been shooting with the villagers. We were on no account allowed to leave the main street. I believe that there were many dead lying behind the houses.

Eventually we crossed the border into Germany at Strasbourg, and from there were transported to Heilbronn by train. We had been on the way for weeks, and fall had come in the meantime. We left Bordeaux in August and arrived in Heilbronn on September 7. While still at the town station in Heilbronn, I learned from an acquaintance that my parents had been informed that I was in a prison camp! How great was our joy when I was reunited with my parents! But we could not remain together for long. All auxiliary air force helpers, of which I was one, had to report for duty again in Stuttgart after only three weeks' leave. We were sent to Dresden and from there on to Jena. There our job was to cover the city with artificial smoke which would conceal the Zeiss camera factory, which was very important in the war effort. All around the city there were hundreds of smoke-making installations. When there was an alarm we had to set them going. Before we came, this job had been done by Russian prisoners of war. As the Russian army approached the German border, the job was assigned to us young German women.

Our superior officer said, "The ladies lived in luxury in Bordeaux. Now they can do some real work for a change!" No consideration was given the hardships we endured during the retreat. Operating the smoke installations was very dangerous. The substance used was acid, which could not be inhaled nor could we allow it to get into our eyes. Once, when the acid got on the face of a colleague, her skin was entirely cauterized. She suffered from its effects for the rest of her life.

We were punished for protesting against this job. We were forced to go through pitch-dark woods and start the smoke installations. Only a short time before that, several Russian prisoners had been housed in the hut allotted to us. We had no water, little to eat. The straw mats on which we were to sleep were old and full of lice. The winter was severe. There had been no news from home for a long time.

News finally did come, of an air raid on Heilbronn and of thirty thousand dead. We were allowed to go home for one week to get news of our relatives. We went by train to Neckarsulm, but had to walk the rest of the way. Standing at the Heilbronn railway station we could do nothing but weep. We walked through the wrecked city over paths of debris and saw the dead shrunken and unrecognizable. This was worse than anything we had experienced so far in the war. It took a long time before we were able to find our relatives, so we stayed in Heilbronn a few days longer than was permitted. When we arrived back in Jena the officer threatened to have us court-martialed.

In March the smoke action was stopped. The front was getting nearer and nearer and most of us were sent home. Because Heilbronn was already occupied, we were sent first to a village near Jena. During the night I heard long columns of people marching past. I sneaked a look out the window and saw a procession of indescribably wretched and miserable people. Their heads were shaved bald, their eyes deep in their sockets, withered forms, no clothes, only gray rags bound round their bodies. They had come from a concentration camp in Thüringen and were to be brought to another camp. Each night a procession like this passed by, and each night it was longer than it had been the night before.

One night I heard two soldiers planning in a whisper to murder their sergeant-major, who was apparently a big tyrant. Those soldiers wanted to take their revenge on him before the war ended. At that time there was no longer any justice, no order, only lynching.

On April 4, 1945, we were relieved of duty and from then on we were civilians. We dyed our uniforms so that the grayish blue of the military uniform could no longer be seen. We hid our identity cards, badges and medals from the oncoming Americans. We hung a white flag of truce out the window and went down into the cellar. The Americans went through the village in tanks. They searched every house and every cellar, but not one shot was fired.

One day an American soldier came and advised us to leave for home as quickly as possible, as the Russian army would be in Jena within a few days. We made ourselves a rucksack out of old rags and exchanged everything we did not urgently need for food. At dawn an old lady from the village showed us the way to the west through the woods. That was on May 2, 1945.

I remember going through the Thüringer Forest and up the Rennsteig without meeting a living soul. The forest was full of munitions installations, and among them lay dead soldiers. A ghastly sight! Once we met a man in shepherd's clothing. He had been a soldier in Austria and wanted to get to Jena where his wife had given birth to a child.

At last we arrived at Heilbronn. The church in Boeckingen, a nearby village, had not been destroyed and we heard its bells ring out four o'clock. We were so touched that we sat down by the side of the road and folded our hands. We were at home at last. It was May 17, 1945.

URSULA SCHULZ

Born in the 1920s. Worked during the war as an accountant for a chocolate factory. Currently a feminist activist working in a center for abused women. Married. Has two daughters.

Standing Helplessly By

In March 1941 I was called up by the RAD [*Reichsarbeitsdienst*] to do obligatory labor for the state as *Arbeitsmädchen* [working girl]. I was placed in Templin, in Uckermark, not far from Berlin. After that assignment was finished, I did obligatory war service as a trained bookkeeper. I was placed in the office of the mayor of Berlin, capital city of the Reich.

By the end of March 1942, I had finished my wartime obligatory service and was able to resume my work at the Trumpf Company's chocolate factory in Weisensee, where I had been happily employed. The managers, Hans and Richard Monheim, were very advanced and provided their workers with many amenities. In the factory complex there was a swimming pool, tennis courts, a large athletic field, and so on. And each week, every one of the 3,300 employees was given "employee goods" — chocolate — which the rest of the population could only dream about. When I returned to the factory I was astonished to find that chocolate production had been reduced by half; in place of chocolate, weapons were being produced — explosives for hand grenades, and much more.

A total of about seven hundred young girls worked in the two departments — chocolate and explosives. They came from Russia and were no more than sixteen or seventeen years old. The way they stood there at those long tables, clothed more or less in rags — it was a pitiful sight. I can still hear their haunting folk songs, so full of homesickness. The official line was that they had come to Germany voluntarily. I knew from my father that they had been forced to come. Their living quarters were at the old racetrack in Weissensee, which my great-grandfather had once helped to build, in makeshift wooden barracks. In the winter they were hard to heat and the occupants were frozen like icicles; in summer they could hardly stand the heat.

I had a chance to see the living situation of the Russian girls firsthand, as a member of the weekly inspection team. Women from the office were sent by the company to the barracks at the racetrack to search for contraband chocolate. The girls were forbidden to eat chocolate and were suspected of stealing some.

There were twelve girls to a barrack, and all the barracks were guarded by Nazis. The sleeping accommodations were tripledecker bunkbeds, with straw pallets and two blankets. The barracks were heated by a potbellied stove. There was no place to cook — that was forbidden. Meals were prepared for them in a field-kitchen. Each one had a dish and utensil (no knives were permitted because of the danger of suicide).

The chocolate company treated the Russians differently from the Germans. The German employees still got a package of chocolate once a week; the Russians were not to be caught eating chocolate. Sometimes some of the packers slipped the girls some chocolate, but no one was supposed to know. Only Germans worked in the section that produced chocolate for the soldiers at the front.

At work we Germans got a free half-liter of cocoa each day for breakfast; the Russian girls got none. I was sick of the cocoa anyway, so I gave mine to one of the Russian girls in such a way that no one could see me do it. Other employees did the same, but I had the bad luck to be caught by the supervisor. He called me every name imaginable. If I didn't want to drink it myself, I should pour it down the drain, he said. If he caught me at it again, we would see each other somewhere else.

The next morning there was an announcement on the bulletin board: "Whoever gives cocoa to the Russians must reckon with a serious penalty." This experience was constantly on my mind, and there was no one that I could talk it over with. Father was far away, and my mother urged me to be cautious, not to endanger her and the children.

In addition to the weekly barracks inspection, as a bookkeeper I had official contact with the Russians when they received their weekly pay envelopes. They were paid much less than us, and a part of their wage was deposited in a closed account. I wasn't able to talk to them. We could only show our compassion with a glance or a smile.

Time and again accidents occurred, especially toward the end of the war. One of the Russians died in an accident, another lost her hand. Many suffered wounds from explosives, as did many German workers. When an explosive detonated, it affected a large area. It was almost a kind of sabotage. The radio was on all day long at work, and some of the Russian girls could understand some German. When the Russian troops reached Berlin, the girls were ecstatic and rushed out to greet their countrymen, never dreaming that they would be regarded as collaborators simply because they had managed to survive in Germany. The fate which awaited them upon their return to the Soviet Union was banishment to Siberia.

Born in 1928, the eldest of four children. Was a member of the Nazi youth organization during the war. After the war worked in the office of a labor union. Is active in the peace movement and believes in non-violence. Married 1950. Has three children.

Blonde Maiden On The Seashore

On September 1, 1939, when World War II began, I was just eleven and a half years old. That summer my parents allowed me to take part in an excursion, lasting several days, with the *Jungmädel* [young girls' organization]. We stayed in a youth hostel in Maulbronn, about thirty miles southwest of Heilbronn. Our group was full of enthusiasm, and most especially we were captivated by our Führer.

Father was a carpenter by trade, following in the footsteps of his father. At the age of forty-two he had been drafted by Organization Todt (OT), a special division responsible for building bridges and doing other engineering projects critical to the German army's success. This division was at the head of the front lines in Russia.

Mother was very bitter about the war. She had been careful not to express her opinion of Hitler, but now she quite openly poured all kinds of abuse upon him, especially during or after a broadcast speech by Hitler, Goebbels or any other Nazi politician. Mother's criticism was seconded by a neighbor who often came over to our house to listen to these speeches over the radio. The two of them didn't make any bones about what they thought of the Nazi regime! Even though I was by nature shy, I vehemently contradicted them — brainwashed *Jungmädel* that I was then.

Toward the end, America's declaration of war on Germany gave occasion for a speech by Hitler, to which we all listened. After our neighbor left, my mother tried to convince me that we would certainly lose the war now that the wealthy United States had joined the fight against us. She said: "Too many hounds are the death of the hare!" I hated that proverb, which Mother had heard from my grandmother and used on many occasions. Probably because I hated that proverb, I became very angry and shouted at my mother: "We would have lost the war long ago if all Germans thought and spoke like you!" Obviously shocked, my mother turned round to the stove and said, more to herself than to me: "One of these days she'll have me put into prison if she continues like this." We had not yet heard of the concentration camps.

The fourteen-year-old girls, after leaving elementary school, had to serve one year of compulsory domestic service. They worked either on the land or in a family with numerous children. Like the other girls in my class, I wanted to serve that year on a farm. I was convinced that by doing so I would be contributing to the victory of Hitler and "Great Germany."

I began my year of service in 1942, on a big farm in Grossgartach, only about six miles from Heilbronn. The farmer and his wife had only one son, Karl. He was nineteen. He was mobilized into the Wehrmacht in 1942, shortly after I arrived. Nothing was ever heard from Karl after he was reported missing in the battle of Stalingrad.

The horses had been confiscated from the farm at the beginning of the war. The farmer, his wife and myself had only oxen to draw the carts as we struggled with thirty acres of field, meadows, vineyards and woods. During the summer of 1942, the army sent soldiers from the nearby anti-aircraft division to help us with the grain and sugar-beet harvest. The following year the soldiers had enough real work to do!

On summer evenings, after the grain had been harvested, the kitchen scrubbed until it glistened, and the milk cans cleaned and polished after they were brought back from the central depot, I was sometimes allowed to go home. On Sundays I was free after the midday meal, but I had to return for the evening meal because there was no food for me at home. Also, I had to bring the milk to the depot.

On the whole, it was a very hard year for me, but one in which I gained a great deal of experience. I received a monthly wage of twelve marks, which was later raised to fifteen marks. Any vacation was out of the question. I spent Sunday afternoons with a friend who was also doing her year of compulsory service. Sometimes we watched as the trains passed continuously from the west to the east, carrying German soldiers from France to Russia. One Sunday we were standing near the railway tracks when a train filled with tanks and guns stopped for a short time. One of the soldiers started a conversation with us. As the train gathered steam to start, the soldier pressed a flier into my hand. It was titled "East Front News." He asked me to write him. He had written his name and address on the flier. We waved until the train was out of sight and then we fell upon the paper. On the cover was a picture of a girl on the beach wearing only a bathing suit. On the other side was a poem which I still remember:

> You blonde girl on the beach
> You make us lose our minds
> Every soldier here is touched and hopes
> that somebody like you still exists.
> We kiss you in thought
> Because you bathe wearing so little
> We envy the photographer
> Because he saw you so sparsely dressed.
> Therefore come again in the East Front Number.
> Do you hear! Today you go bathing alone,
> But one day, we'll say goodbye to Russia — you will see —
> and I will come to you by the sea!

The soldier's name was Hans Wartmann. I wrote him that same day, but I never received a reply.

After I completed my year of compulsory service, my mother went with me to the labor exchange to look for an apprenticeship. I had firmly resolved to become a fashion designer. If that was not possible, I thought I could become interested in working as an interior decorator. I had an aptitude for handicrafts.

Upon entering the office in which vocational advice was given, we exchanged the obligatory "Heil Hitler" greeting. My mother was allowed to sit down, but I had to remain standing. The lady who was to advise me asked me what type of work I wished to pursue, to which I replied "fashion designer." After a period of silence, I was asked: "Have you any other intentions?" Rather embarrassed, I answered in the affirmative.

"Well?" she asked.

"Interior decorator," I answered softly.

At that the lady burst into loud laughter and said to her colleague, seated at the other side of the office: "Did you hear that, Fräulein Miller? She wants to become a fashion designer or an interior decorator. Doesn't that make you laugh yourself sick?" She turned to us again and, still amused but in a stern voice, said: "You'd better get all that nonsense out of your head. I'll tell you what kind of women the Führer needs now!" And then she enumerated: "Nurses, bee-keepers, fish breeders and animal breeders." After a brief pause: "What would you like best?" I shook my head timidly. "Well, then it would be best if you were to get married as quickly as possible and have a few children. That would serve the Fuhrer's purpose too."

This was followed by an embarrassing silence. Looking into my report book, the woman then said: "Well, if you have no idea of what you want to be, you'd better work in an office." She then filled out a card of introduction, pushed it into my mother's hand, and opened the door for us.

Thus began my commercial training in the office of a well-known Heilbronn business. I was assigned to a suburban branch office where I worked under a boss who was truly a despot. Working hours were from seven in the morning until noon, and from one to six. Saturdays we worked from seven-thirty to twelve-thirty.

For weeks we had received no mail from my father. Often I would arrive home and find my mother sitting in the kitchen weeping. We had never had to wait for such a long time for a letter from Father. Mother decided to write to the wives of several of Father's comrades in hopes of getting news of him through them. Still we were not able to determine his fate or his whereabouts. Finally, one day a notice arrived from Berlin that Father had been officially reported missing. Somewhat later a letter arrived from a comrade of Father's saying that they had been together constructing a bridge for a retreat and had been fired on by the Russian artillery. Father had probably been killed. This sorrowful event put a damper on my patriotism and my enthusiasm for the Führer for a short time. However, I was told by the wife of my former teacher: "You ought to be proud that your father has died a hero's death for the Führer and our Fatherland."

In September 1945 we received word, quite unexpectedly, that my father would be coming home. He had been detained in a Russian prison camp and he was not dead. He was brought from Russia to the German border in one of the first transports to travel between the Russian and the U.S. occupation zones. From there, he, along with several others, was taken by the Americans to Heidelberg where he was given the necessary official papers stating his right to travel.

Father was barefoot and carried his heavy wooden clogs in one hand. He had lost one eye, his hair had turned completely white, and he was as thin as a skeleton. Meeting him at the edge of our village, we took him into our arms.

Born 1916. Was in the German army during the war. Fiancé and brother were killed in action. Worked as an actress and as an office clerk after the war. Is active in the peace movement. Divorced. Has one son.

1942

1985

It Must Never Happen Again!

*H*ow did I go through World War II?

At the beginning I was a bit anxious and uneasy. But I was young and carefree, so I did not worry too much. My father was in his late fifties and was therefore not mobilized. My brother had just graduated from high school and was given the opportunity to study meteorology in a student corps. The knowledge thus gained was to be put into use later for the army.

The days passed as they had always done, except that food was rationed and we could get clothing only with a supply ticket. The press and the broadcasting system were censored. The information given over the radio spoke only of military victories, and we were proud of our soldiers as we had been taught to be.

And the persecution of the Jews? Of course we heard of the Reich's "Crystal Night," the breaking and splintering of the shop windows in Jewish stores and the burning down of the synagogues. But wasn't it possible we had really been exploited by the Jews? There were no ordinary workers among them. They were all university graduates, artists or flourishing tradesmen. They dominated the economy. We "Aryans," members of the Germanic race, were to keep our blood "pure," for "Providence" (a favorite word of Hitler's) had determined that we were to bring our culture to other peoples — especially to the Eastern barbarians — and to rule over them.

We were a "people without space" [*Volk ohne Raum*]. With the motto "You are nothing, your nation is everything," an ardent patriotism was instilled into us. We sang folk songs on our hikes on Sundays. These told of the love of nature and of our home. Neither I nor my girlfriends were interested in politics. We didn't even take the trouble to read Hitler's book *Mein Kampf* [My Struggle]. Instead we met together in a private literary circle and listened breathlessly to what Knut Hamsun wrote about love. We were carried away by the melancholia in Rilke's diary. Now and again we attended big public demonstrations. It was such a solemn occasion when the flag was raised to the sound of the German national anthem or the "Horst-Wessel Song" amid a scene of innumerable flaming torches.

The National Socialist idea is pathetic and sentimental, and our young naïve hearts were entirely open to it. We had been brought up never to criticize or express our own opinion. At school, at home and at work, only orders and obedience to those orders existed. We didn't realize that we were quietly and gradually being molded to an inner readiness for war.

This became especially clear during our year of compulsory service. It was my first taste of living communally, and I adapted to it very well. Our schedule was something like this: Call to get up at 6:15 A.M., early-morning exercise, singing, breakfast. Then eight hours of work with farmers. Depending on the season, we spread dung on the fields or harvested potatoes and turnips, threshed, etc. In our free time something was either read or told to us. We acted plays or we recited poems: "I will crush all the flowers in my heart / Only one shall live: Deutschland."

The weekly newspaper report, which had to be written by an *Arbeitsmädchen* [young girl in compulsory service] from reports in the six daily newspapers, was a purely political activity. Civil war was raging in Spain. Influenced by the Nazi press, we sympathized with the brave General Franco and we hoped that the war would soon end in a victory for him.

Saluting the flag was an especially solemn rite, for which we had to wear our uniforms. Everything went according to a strict ritual. We formed a circle around the flagpole and while saluting with our right hand, we sang one of our patriotic songs which went something like this: "Let the banners wave in the glorious dawn that lights a new victory or burns into death. For if we die, like a tower is our seed. A folk has hundreds of heirs and dies hundreds of times." Then two of us left the circle to raise or to lower the colors according to the time of day — morning or evening.

Our camp was small and so we were one big family. Our camp leader was hardly older than we were. We were charmed by her fine profile and her reserved grace. We fell over ourselves in our efforts to please her. Once, when she observed that she was behind schedule with her office work, we pressed her to allow us to help her.

After several months the camp was broken up and we were sent to a larger camp. After a short train journey and a fairly long march, we were standing on an icy cold day in front of the entrance to the barracks. At the right and the left of the gate stood an *Arbeits-mädchen* shouldering a big spade and without gloves! That was the regulation. Our turn would come too, we were told, and someone had to stand guard all through the night. But then, at midnight, when a ghostly procession — people dressed in long white sheets, carrying lighted skulls and singing bloodcurdling songs — passed through the dormitory, we realized that they had been playing jokes on the new ones.

Here there was military drill. Our new camp leader was, in both tone and carriage, like a sergeant-major, but she was fair. We had to sing and keep strictly in line when marching, and sometimes we were called in the middle of the night to march silently. But there was a wonderful comradeship. Many of my comrades come vividly to mind today: Mia, a ballet dancer with lithe movements, who wore a corset day and night to keep slim, and who had a pathetic affection for a young man we called Spitzmaus [shrew mouse], a simple factory worker; Langnese, the 200% worker, who caught us once as we were going to the toilet direct from the flag ritual — when we were still in uniform — and made a dreadful scene; and Lotte, who was always making jokes and who could imitate animals and birds so well — especially a hen who had just laid an egg. She generally "performed" before we went to bed, and while we were still laughing over her jokes she fell asleep in her bed and was snoring.

The economy was booming. No more emergency orders, less unemployment. Highways were built, the Volkswagen, which every German was said to be able to afford, was put on the market. Hitler stopped payment of the reparation debts from World War I. Thanks to *"Kraft durch Freude"* [Strength through Happiness], it was for the first time possible for the average worker to go away on vacation. There was also success in international politics — the annexation of Austria and Czechoslovakia.

During the first two years of the war I worked in a hardware store, making out invoices for nine hours a day. I continued adding up figures in my head even during the night! We had no calculating machines at that time. The head clerk asked me after each telephone call: "Have you got the reference number?" — for iron and other metals were rationed at that time. A few yards away from me sat the Nazi branch leader [*Ortsgruppenleiter*], who spent the greater part of the working hours talking on the telephone with his Party friends. He was neither friendly nor generous toward us girls in the invoice department. It was very difficult to change jobs at that time.

It was here that I was faced for the first time with a soldier's death. Hanni, who sat directly opposite me, came to the office one morning as pale as death and with eyes swollen and red from weeping. It grieved my heart to see her suffering so terribly — she who had so often made remarks full of humor to break the monotony of the working day. "Christl?" I asked. She nodded mechanically. I found no words of comfort. There are none. Only a very short time before, she had told me of her and Christl's love and plans for a future together, and also that he was in her thoughts every second of the day. Her life was ruined, for she was not one who could change over from one to the other. On December 4, 1944 [the date of the firebombing of Heilbronn], her physical life also came to an end.

Spring 1942. Our soldiers were far into Russia. Wanting to leave home I volunteered for service in the East and was sent to Riga [Latvia] for duty in the supply office of the Reich ministry there. The work was not uninteresting. I had a lot of contact with people. The newcomers were supplied with furniture, household goods and uniforms from my office. A Jew was employed in the clothing department and he often amused and cheered us with his charm, humor and his witty answers. He wore his Star of David with composure, as though he knew nothing of the danger he was in. One morning there was a tumult in the clothing department and I heard an excited man's voice shouting: "What — by a Jew!? That is the absolute limit! I am supposed to have my uniform tried on by a Jew!!" Aversion and horror could be heard in his voice, as if he were being forced to deal with a nauseating reptile. "I'll complain. I'll phone Berlin today."

In the evening there were often parties, even dances were consciously encouraged in order to raise the morale of the troops. Riga was only a communication zone. Officers and men were generally only there for a short period of convalescence. We felt little of the war there. Only the colorful street picture with various uniforms, the miserable display of goods in the shop windows and the crowded streetcars with people hanging like grapes on the runningboard reminded us that we were not living in normal times.

I got to know Susanne in the anteroom of Doctor V., one of the most important men of the Third Reich commissary. She was the ideal person — because of her good humor, her ladylike behavior and, not least, her intelligence. She lived with a friend in a large apartment, situated in the center of the town. The rest of us lived in a girls' hostel, in small rooms with standard furniture and an ice-cold shower. Susanne often had guests, all of whom were pleasant, interesting people. Wherever they came from — from the trenches, from enemy flights or from hospital — they always found warmth, happiness and understanding with her. They seldom spoke about the war. They enjoyed the warm comfort, lived only one day at a time and neither spoke nor thought of the morrow until they had to go out again to be enveloped in cold, darkness and danger.

In summer I spent the weekends with Susanne at the seaside. Nowhere was there a sky with such strange colors as the sky over the Bay of Riga — from a delicate lilac to dark purple. It was amusing to see the men of that region go down to the beach in a procession, dressed in their pajamas as was their custom. "Enjoy war. Peace will be terrible," was one of our frivolous mottos when, once again, we had pleasantly spent a sunny day.

Once, on a long hike, we had lost our way. Our feet hurt badly and there was nobody around to show us the way. There was no streetcar either. At last a horse-cart passed. At last! We waved and it came nearer and stopped. But then the coachman heard us speaking German and away he went, as if he'd seen a ghost.

Jews were employed in the German store. My boss had given me some textile ration tickets — illegally — and I wanted to buy some material to make a coat. The saleslady was a really beautiful middle-aged Jewess. The tears rolled slowly down her cheeks as she spoke of her great fear. I was embarrassed and felt helpless as I tried to comfort her and give her courage — words which I myself did not really believe. "You are needed here. Wait till the war is over. Then everything will be better." Turning my head, I saw in a corner a stand full of worn women's clothes — supposedly coming from Jewesses. As I left the store I could feel the dark, knowing eyes fixed on me. Had I not heard of shootings a short time before? The Jews had to dig their own graves before the executions. I was horrified by such cruelty.

Shortly after, I witnessed a similar hideous atrocity. One morning I heard shots in front of the office window. When I went outside I saw a man's body lying face downwards on the sidewalk, blood streaming to the edge of the street from under him. Beside him stood an officer from the SD [*Sicherheitsdienst*—Security Service], a revolver still in his hand, shouting in an enraged voice: "The pig wanted to shoot me dead!" There lay the Jew who had passed our office every day on the way to his place of work. The SD-man tried to justify himself: "I asked him why, being a Jew, he wasn't wearing his Star of David. Then he put his hand in his pocket." Ashamed, we stood there, but not one of us said what was certainly evident: How could one assume that the Jew had a pistol?

One day I received a letter from my employer. I was to be sent to Schaulen. No explanation was given — only a few lines. Annoyed, I went to the personnel office. I didn't want to leave Riga. I had been trained there, and my friends were there too. The staff manager was no help. He shouted at me: "What do you expect me to do? Am I responsible? Did I suggest the change?"

All sorts of things went through my head. My "sins" passed before my eyes. Was it the textile ration tickets, which had helped me to get a warm coat, or had they discovered that I had signed an authorization which enabled a Latvian colleague to escape service in the German army? I made no reply to the staff manager and took leave. The last thing I wanted to do was to further irritate him.

Schaulen was a miserable little town, but the work was versatile and interesting. I was responsible for the organization of the educational system, but I also had to help when necessary in the department of legal affairs, for we had a great number of acts of sabotage committed by the natives of the area. A woman wrote that her husband was "at the end of his tether" and we would do well to dismiss him; he had disrupted the telephone wires.

Once when I returned from home-leave I found that my wardrobe had been broken into, and that only a few wrinkled, creased and stained clothes and a torn belt were left in it. I knew immediately which one of my fellow-occupants was to blame, but there was little sense in my reporting her. She could afford to be late for work in the morning; it was said that she was the girlfriend of the personnel manager.

Night air raid alert in Schaulen. The Russian air raids are harmless, they said, and there was no shelter anywhere. All of a sudden it became as bright as broad daylight outside, the "Christmas trees" which we were so much afraid of, appeared in the sky. The planes came roaring along — nearer and nearer. We ran in panic from the house onto an open field and then farther, until we found a tree under which we could take shelter. A young housewife screamed and moaned: "My child! my child!" She had left her child in the house! At last it was all over. From afar we could hear the detonation of the bombs.

I first met Achim at a birthday party given for an elderly colleague. It was like a miracle. What I had just thought, he expressed in words — and vice versa. It was understood that we would marry later, and we made plans for the future. Happy hours followed, filled with accord, harmony, tenderness. Others were full of anxiety and foreboding, for Achim's unit was soon to be sent to the front.

On the day of his departure Achim was depressed. "If I have to leave now I shall never come back. I feel it," he said. Achim loved poetry just as I do. Our volume of poems lay open on the table in front of us, at a poem by Ina Seidel, called "Lamentation of a Young Woman," in which a young girl laments: "Young men fallen in battle / have made young girls brides of death instead of mothers."

We were together for the last time between three and four A.M. at the station in Schaulen. We hardly felt the biting February cold. A whistle, the train goes off. Achim's beloved face fades more and more in the darkness and the steam of the engine. "Dear God, let him come back to me!"

Six weeks later, Saturday morning. I should have been on duty but a bad cold kept me at home. "What is my supervisor doing here in my flat?" I asked myself, when I saw him at the door. He had an exceedingly earnest look on his face and a letter in his hand. It was my letter — my letter to Achim. On the front of the envelope was the following remark written in red ink: "1. Killed in battle for Great Germany. 2. Return to Sender."

"Pain can reach the heart only drop by drop" were the words of Otto Gmelin, a popular author at that time. It hit me like a blow from a club. Pain, despair, anger — and yes, even hate. What right had the government to send young men to their death — to destroy happiness? Firstly, secondly, in red ink! The way was laid for my future engagement in the peace movement.

The end of July, 1944. The Soviets were approaching. We could hear the machine guns from afar. It was high time to leave to go westward. We spent the night hidden in a hayloft, and the following day a train was standing ready for our departure. The train with its hard wooden benches often stopped for hours for no apparent reason, and mostly at night. We longed for a warm soft bed. Suddenly, when once again the train stopped on a sidetrack in the late evening, two railway employees came toward us. Would we — my colleague and I — like to sleep for one night in their beds? They were on night duty. We accepted gratefully. But oh — oh what a smell! The sheets had probably not been changed for months. Overtired, we fell into a deep sleep until — it was still dark — we were brutally called out of our sleep: "The train is leaving!" Never did we get on our feet so quickly!

We spent the night in Koenigsberg. I had become separated from the others in the meantime. Air-raid alert. I ran out onto the street, for there was no air-raid shelter in the hotel. I was told that there was a shelter in the movie house. I had hardly reached the theatre when the first bombs fell. Again and again the hissing whistle and the thundering blow. Would it hit us? The air in the shelter was stifling. The old man on the wooden chair began gasping for breath and coughing. His wife whimpered, "Joshie, keep calm, keep calm. Where have you put your drops?" At last the bombing calmed down. Would we be able to get out of the shelter? I climbed up and opened the flap of the trapdoor. High blazing flames everywhere! A sea of fire. Clearly, we had better stay where we were. Time seemed an eternity. At last I took off my coat, dipped it into a full barrel of water, wrung it out and then put it on. Outside, the flames were still knee-high and the skeletons of houses stood like ghosts staring up at the sky. There was a pool of water near the manor house. There was air to breathe there and crowds of people rushed in that direction. For the rest of the night I slept on the couch with kindly people who were total strangers. The following day I caught one of the last trains going west — toward home.

October 1944, Heilbronn. The employment agency and the total war brought my short breathing spell to an end. It was either work in an ammunition factory or the army. I went as helper in the army, in the Taunus. There was good comradeship among the "little people," but a strict hierarchy was maintained among the officers. The most humane and best-liked superior officer was a NS officer of high rank. The view he took of National Socialism and his belief in the "final victory" gave way increasingly to bitter disillusion.

In Taunus there was a lot of snow and sunshine in the winter of 1944-45, and we soon found out where we could rent skis and where the most suitable ski runs were. Our midday break was extended until four P.M. but in exchange we worked until late at night.

Here too we could hear the thundering of the big guns, but eventually we got used to that. A happy feeling gradually came over us. Sometimes from the hall or the stairs we heard singing or whistling coming from the officers' mess. An order appeared on the board in the officers' quarters. It read: "Singing and whistling in the officers' quarters is strictly forbidden!" That evening we laughed at the words someone had added to this order: "Where people sing is the place to stay. Only nasty people have no songs to sing." The culprit was soon found and given three days of solitary confinement.

Thus, at last, she had time for her private correspondence!

January 1945. Short news from Heilbronn. My brother had been killed in action. After years of study he had, in the autumn of 1944, been drafted as a parachutist. My brother, whose closest friend and confidante I had been, had to die a useless death in a war which had long since been lost. Months later, after the war had ended, I learned the bitter truth. During his assignment in Luxembourg his face had been completely shattered by a shell. His clear, honest face with the mocking, grimacing mouth when he made jokes about the Führer and his motto ("You are the guarantee for our future") as my father gazed at his favorite son while anxiously looking around to see if anyone was within earshot and hissed: "Be quiet!" How long could he have lain there in a pool of blood, maimed — and how many others had there been before him? Perhaps his shrill cry of pain sounded from his shattered mouth and echoed unheard until, at last, liberating death came to that lonely creature. Father showed me his last letter: "Don't grieve if I never return." He too had a premonition of death.

Born in 1911, in London. Grew up in England, then worked as an *au pair* in France and Algeria. Currently lives in Germany. Married twice. Has one son.

1940

A Young Englishwoman

I was born on September 3, 1911, in London. My father was a German, but he had lived for many years in England — neglecting, however, to become naturalized. My mother was English. In 1914 my father was given the choice of being interned or of emigrating. In 1915 we emigrated to the United States, where we lived — in New Orleans and in New York — until my father's death in 1925, when my mother and I returned to England.

In 1930 I went, without my mother, to France. Being English, I was never given a worker's permit in France and I therefore had to work as an *au pair* girl in various families. In 1932 I went to Algiers, as an *au pair* with a French family. I stayed there for five years, until

I married my first husband — actually only to obtain French citizenship! — and went to live on his family's small farm in Alsace, about seven kilometers from the German frontier.

Because my marriage was exceedingly unhappy I had decided to leave my husband and return to England. But I agreed to help on the farm in August and leave for England on September 1, 1939. Unfortunately, German troops marched into Poland on that date, whereupon France immediately declared war on Germany. Our village, which was very near the frontier, had to be evacuated immediately. The cattle were driven out of the stables and left to their fate. The farmers quickly packed what they thought was most essential and we all started off by horse and cart from Sundhouse, our village. We were on the road all night until we reached our temporary destination, the village of Rapoltsweiler (in French it is called "Ribeauville") in the Vosges. We stayed there for three days, after which we were packed into cattle trucks and transported to the Dordogne, in the center of France.

There was naturally much confusion and a lot of quarrels and brawls in the cattle trucks, because everybody's nerves were strained to the utmost. There was no sanitation; we could not wash ourselves. From time to time the doors were opened and Red Cross workers brought us food and drink and we could go to the toilet. I did not, for private reasons, stay at the refugee camp in the Dordogne, but went on to Cannes where I found work as a French-English teacher in a private school.

In 1940, when France had almost completely capitulated in the war against the Germans, Italy declared war on France, and Nice was evacuated. Not so Cannes. However, all foreigners, especially Jews, left Cannes as quickly as possible and there was nothing left for me to do but to return to the Dordogne.

When the farmers in the Dordogne heard that the Germans were in Paris and marching southward, they were filled with a terrible fear. Some of them even hid in the woods. The Alsatians, however, were not afraid. They hoped for better organization by the Germans — and they could speak German! The Germans had the Alsatians sent back home to Alsace — this time not in cattle trucks, but in nice railway coaches! The Alsatians were happy! At all Alsatian railway stations garlands had been hung bearing the words: "Welcome to German Alsace!" We were given dried-bean soup and German was spoken. As I could not speak German at that time, somebody translated for me that the German army would, in about two weeks' time, have conquered England too. You can imagine how I felt! The Germans' problem in my case was whether to have me interned as an English national, or to send me to do forced labor in Germany. They decided on the latter.

I was sent with a transport to Salem. I was very thin at that time, so nobody wanted me as a laborer and I stood for a long time with the others—we were like cattle at a market. But I was finally taken on as cleaning help in the Schloss-Schule — a very elite boarding school. I had to work about thirteen hours a day, and as I was awkward and could not speak German I was mocked by all the German workers. When I did anything wrong, immediately someone would shout at me: "Dirty Frenchwoman!" The enmity of the German charwomen was made very clear to me.

I had to share a room with five German servants. I still had a few chocolates from France, which I shared with my roommates. Chocolate had not been available for a very long time in Germany (their motto was: "Cannons are better than butter"). But when one of the girls had a birthday and managed to get some candy, she went round the room, giving a piece to each girl until she came to me. She stopped and said very plainly that she had no candy for a "dirty Frenchwoman!"

They often played the harmonica and sang until late in the night, but when I wanted to join in they immediately shouted: "Shut your mouth!" I wanted to learn German and had procured books for that purpose, but when I wanted to use them the light was immediately put out. Finally an Alsatian woman went to the head of housekeeping and reported on how I was being tormented. I was then given another room with two sisters, who were both mentally retarded. It is true that they did not annoy or threaten me, but I had to be on the lookout all the time, since they stole like magpies!

I was always abused about my work. I could never do anything right. In the afternoon when we had to be in the kitchen and peel a certain quota of potatoes, a German helper always came and snatched my knife away so that I had to try to find another one, which prevented me from fulfilling my quota.

I was very badly treated in Salem, but there were very few Nazis there. It so happened that I once attended a Bible study group in my free time, as I was beginning to understand German fairly well. There I met Mrs. H., who was a true Christian woman and had the great courage to invite me to her home even though she met with much resistance within her family. Through her acquaintance and her friendship, my position with the servants in the Schloss-Schule greatly improved. They still picked on me, but somehow I was no longer a heap of dirt.

Once I was asked for a contribution destined for the construction of Stukas (dive bombers) to be used in air raids in the Battle of Britain. I could do nothing but cry bitterly, whereupon a student took pity on me and spoke with the chief housekeeper. She was very understanding, and I was excused from having to give a contribution. After eighteen months I was allowed to leave Salem to go and be "harvest help" on my husband's farm. I never returned.

As I had learned German so well, I was sent to Stuttgart to act as interpreter for the other French workers — in addition to my other job as a cleaner at the M-Hotel in Stuttgart. The director of the hotel was a big Nazi. All of his speeches — and there were very many of them — ended with the words: "And remember, the English are our greatest enemies! Heil Hitler!"

At the beginning everything went well for me at the M-Hotel. A woman pastry cook from the eastern part of Berlin worked there in the bakery and she always took my side. She had been a communist since her childhood and she helped me in many a dangerous situation.

In Stuttgart I soon made the acquaintance of a group of French people who formed a "resistance" in their own way. We felt strong when we were together, and so we spent as much time as possible with one another. We met in the evenings, in the old huts in which the French workers — mostly prisoners of war — were lodged. Stuttgart was veiled in artificial fog in the evenings because of the danger of air raids, and this made it much easier for us to hold our secret gatherings. Through our resistance group I got to know my second husband, who was a French prisoner of war but was treated like a foreign worker. He was a typographer and was allowed to practice his profession in the Klett printing works.

As the French were not considered an "inferior race" as were, for example, the Poles and the Russians, they did not have to be shut up in camps and were allowed a certain amount of freedom. When their daily work was finished they were allowed to stay together without the presence of a guard. But it often happened that Frenchmen were turned over to the Gestapo for quite insignificant offenses.

* * *

Once we were told that the *Arbeitsamt* [official employment agency] needed a certain number of people for the ammunition factory. Spontaneously I said to a German colleague: "I hope I'm not among them!" A few days later as I was about to start work I was met by the director, who shouted and screamed at me. As far as I could make out, it was his "sacred duty" to report me to the Gestapo because I had refused to work for the "German Victory!" Finally he unintentionally disclosed the name of the colleague to whom I had made the remark, at which point I knew what this was all about.

After a fervent but silent prayer, I asked him if *he* would like to help make bombs to kill his own mother? (My mother was in England.) He seemed to understand my argument and dismissed me with various warnings.

Later I had to work in a factory where I was told over and over again that the V-bombs we made were to be used to destroy England. I slept in the hut-camp where the French prisoners were lodged. In February 1944, the whole complex was burned to the ground during an air raid. We were rescued, and the French prisoners rebuilt the camp as best they could. But I was no longer able to stay there.

About this time I was expecting my first child, and my future husband's employer came to my rescue. He offered to have me registered with his firm along with the other French workers, so that I could get food ration cards and have a roof over my head. From then on we listened more and more to the forbidden foreign radio stations. Mr. K. listened with us. He was certainly not a Nazi!

Being pregnant and French I was entitled to an extra distribution of fruit juice, but when I went to fetch the ration I was greeted with: "Heil Hitler!" I turned around and left without my fruit juice! My baby was born in June, in the maternity clinic. After three weeks my baby had to be taken to a children's hospital; he had a stomach ailment and could not keep down any nourishment.

From July 25-30, Stuttgart was continually bombed and almost entirely destroyed. We spent every night in utter darkness in the cellar, which rocked with the force of the bombs. The French workers were all loyal to Mr. K and always tried to extinguish the fires caused by the incendiary bombs and thus save the works.

While my child was in clinic I had to walk there and back every day to deliver my mother's milk to save my baby's and other babies' lives. It was a long walk — it took about two hours each way — and was dangerous because of the unexploded bombs that lay about. Each day as I made the long walk I could never be sure that the clinic had not been bombed overnight or that my child was still alive.

My husband, being Alsatian, was mobilized by the Germans in 1945, but he refused to fight for them. He did not heed the mobilization order, and Mr. K. tried to prove that he was urgently needed by the firm. This argument was not accepted and we were warned by the Wehrmacht that if Edouard did not report for duty he would be executed. So Mr. K. hid us — thus endangering his own life — in a cellar. The French workers brought us our food and there we stayed — with the baby, who had in the meantime been discharged from the clinic — until the French entered Stuttgart and liberated us.

Mr. K. asked us to stay in Stuttgart and help him during his "denazification." He had been forced to join the National Socialist Party or else have his printing works confiscated by the Party. He promised us living quarters once Stuttgart was rebuilt. At the time we were living in a ruin. My husband decided to stay with the firm and I translated piles of denazification certificates. All German adults who were able to handle a shovel were made to carry off the debris left by the air raid.

The winter of 1946-47 was bitter cold and there was very little food available. There was little or no fuel or insulation material, and some children literally froze in their beds. The windows and the walls glistened with frost. Unfortunately, Mr. K. was killed in a car accident in 1951, so we did not get our promised dwelling until much later.

Wishes to remain anonymous.

Persecution

We were Jehovah's Witnesses and our religion pro-
hibited us from participating in military service. My husband was
arrested early in 1938 by the military police, for not reporting, as ordered, for military duty. He was first imprisoned in Heilbronn, and
later was transferred to the prison in Neckarsulm. I could almost
look into his cell from our living room window.

There were very few Jehovah's Witnesses in Neckarsulm. We
were not officially persecuted, but my son was not given any school-
books as were the other children. For a long time nobody would give
me a job because of my religion.

We learned to tolerate people pointing at us and saying "There, look at them, the Jehovah's Witnesses." Our Church stuck together and its members helped each other out. The baker was a Jehovah's Witness and gave me a job in the bakery, as well as food. On occasion, I got a little money from our church.

Most of the time, Jehovah's Witnesses do not vote, so election days were always especially difficult for us. At that time we stayed away from people. Often we would go to the woods so our neighbors would not find us at home if they came looking for us. Once, twenty-two men came to collect us to make us go and vote. Among them was my own brother. We weren't angry with him, because we knew that it was the time of persecution, as it says in the Bible. We had to hold all our meetings secretly, constantly changing locations, so that no one knew exactly where we met. We were always afraid of getting caught. Some of our members stayed away, because they could no longer stand the fear.

We Jehovah's Witnesses have never done anything against the state. We wanted to keep ourselves out of everything. Our faith contradicted that which the government expected from us. That was the reason for the persecution.

My husband was released from prison in 1939, and in September of that same year war broke out. On October 5 my husband was sent back to prison. This time they took him to Berlin. His trial was held on November 1. At seven in the evening of November 10 he was told that he should write to me. That was his last letter. He was executed at daybreak. It took a while before I got his letter. My brother-in-law thought I should have gone to Berlin to be with my husband, or to persuade him to renounce his faith in order to save his life. But I believed it would have been too late. As it is written in the Bible, many have lost their lives because of their faith.

Other Jehovah's Witnesses who renounced their faith in prison were not sentenced to death but were sent to the front lines to fight, and in the end they received the same punishment.

[Frau S. never received an official notification informing her of the execution of her husband in Ploetzensee, where many resisters were executed. In his last letter he wrote that he expected his death the next morning. This letter is all she has. On behalf of Frau S. the Heilbronn Women for Peace asked the administration of Ploetzensee to check the files of 1939 in order to officially confirm the execution of Mr. S. We were told that the administration is not authorized to give out any information about that time.]

Born 1927. Married and has one son.

A Child From Berlin

In 1933 Adolf Hitler became Chancellor. I was six years old and had just started school, near where we lived, in the densely populated inner city of Berlin. I grew up during the time when Hitler's National Socialist Party was in power. We children were captivated by the long torchlight processions, the mass parades and mass meetings. People crowded together at the Wilhelmsplatz in front of the Chancery of the Reich, shouting in unison "We want to see the Führer!" This was a period of mass hysteria without equal. Everywhere one could see the words: "Führer, command! We will follow!" And people did follow, even into death. Seldom has it happened that a people have been so manipulated into war.

In BDM [*Band Deutscher Mädchen* — Organization of German Girls] stories were read to us which prepared us for war. One of these stories remains especially clear in my memory: a group of soldiers is advancing into enemy territory. Their path leads through a swamp. It is nighttime and nobody is allowed to speak. Suddenly a soldier falls and is in danger of drowning. None of his comrades notice the accident. In order not to endanger the others with his cries for help, he presses his face on the surface of the water and slowly drowns.

Just before the outbreak of the war, I spent my school vacation with relatives on a farm in Pomerania, on the Polish border. While playing in a meadow, I noticed a shed hidden in a thicket of shrubs. My aunt had strictly forbidden us children from going anywhere near it. It was only much later that I learned that ammunition and rifles were being stored there. Just before the attack on Poland, soldiers came during the night and cleared out the shed.

At the end of the war, when the village was taken over by the Poles, my aunt was one of the few Germans to remain. As punishment for her complicity with the German army, she was forced to till the fields by dragging a heavy plow as if she were a horse.

Few changes were noticeable during the first year of the war. When blackouts were first ordered, my father and us children made covers out of black paper which we hung over the windows every evening. Electric bulbs in the streetlamps and on the staircase were painted dark blue. When we left the house in the evening, we put luminous badges on our clothes so that we could be seen. Streetcars and automobiles had black paper stuck over their headlights.

Everybody received a food ration card. Workers and children had special cards, called A&X, which allowed them more food from the one grocer, butcher and baker with whom we were registered. Hoarding of goods not yet rationed was strictly forbidden. Children were supposed to spy on their parents, and we three children were radiant with happiness when we found several packages of washing powder that had been hidden by my mother in the kitchen. We sang comic songs as we piled the cartons up on the table in the living room. Even today I am still ashamed of myself for that act. But when my mother came home she only laughed and hid everything again, better than she had before.

I remember the first air raid. It took place in the daytime. The first detonation sounded like a clap of thunder. It destroyed a big apartment house, so that all that remained was a smoking mountain of rubble. We could hear the people trapped inside and tried for hours to get them free. When in the evening the city sank into darkness, gigantic reflectors were set up and their ghostly light could be seen from afar.

Digging continued through the night. When those who had been buried in that dark hole were finally taken out, they were all dead. Unnerved by the first air raid, I could not hide my fear during the next one. I could not stop shaking with fear. I was thirteen years old and I wanted to live.

In 1940 orders were given to evacuate children to the country. My school was given a wonderful old castle in Semmering, Austria. There we lived for nine months without an air raid. In the beginning of April 1941, the fat Field Marshal Göring moved into the elegant Panhans Hotel in Semmering. It was from there that he directed the sudden attack on Yugoslavia. Although no official comment was made about it, we learned also of Germany's invasion of Russia, which was launched on June 22. We children were all very homesick and were glad when, in the autumn of 1941, we were allowed to return home.

When I returned to Berlin, my father was away in the army. My brother was drafted immediately after his high school graduation. After a brief training period he had a short breathing space during which he remained in a military hospital in Berlin, where he was treated for scarlet fever. We were very happy and thankful for that short respite before he received orders to go to Russia. He was given a few hours of home leave. I remember he was very serious and spoke little. I could feel his fear. After saying our goodbyes we watched as he turned around the bend in the street. After that we received a number of letters from him. When his letters came we were always overjoyed. But then no more letters arrived for a very long time. In despair my parents wrote to his unit.

The day came when, in the late afternoon, our doorbell rang. A messenger from the Party, dressed in civilian clothes, stood at our door with a serious expression on his face and asked to speak to my mother. Knowing already what he would say, Mother sent me into another room. The stranger did not have much to say, but gave my mother a letter from a Lieutenant Colonel Steinhoff, informing her that my brother had been reported missing and there was little hope of his being alive. My mother never showed any emotion or tears in our presence. She moved about with a petrified expression and did her housework with an air of hysteria. At night we heard as she cried in utter despair. She never gave up the hope of his return. The year before her death, in 1983, she applied again to the Red Cross for news of him.

Toward the end of the war, sirens wailed almost every evening as air-raid attacks increased. Mechanically we would pick up our air-raid bags. They held our most important papers, warm clothing and some food. Before leaving the house we would open the windows just a little, as a means of preventing the glass panes from shattering. Beds had been set up in the shelter so that we could lie down if the air raid or the alert lasted for a long time. If the all-clear signal came after ten P.M., which was often the case, school began one hour later the following day. At school the teachers fully understood our fatigue. We were not happy children and we did not play any pranks.

Food rations had dwindled. My mother, who was continually trying to fill our hungry mouths, baked cake from potatoes. One day she dragged a big carton of elderberries home. We ate elderberries in every conceivable form — jam, soup and cake; there was no end.

The surrender came at the end of April, 1945. I think it was the 26th. Standing at the window and looking down on the street below, I saw the first Russian soldier. A woman waving a white flag of truce hurried toward him and shook his hand. We picked up our air-raid bags and all the tenants from our building assembled in the shelter, as had been agreed upon before. We remained there for three days and nights, as fighting was still going on. The Russians who came into the cellar from time to time could speak only three words of German: "Uri" (wristwatch) in the daytime, and that ill-famed "Frau come!" in the night. The first time I heard "Frau come," I was awakened from a deep sleep. A Russian soldier standing at the foot of my bed pointed at me. I refused to go with him. My mother stood up in a menacing fashion, and a child in our corner began to cry. The soldier strolled past me when a middle-aged woman sacrificed herself by offering to go with him. I sat terrified in my upper berth. My heart was beating violently and sleep was out of the question. The following night I was unrecognizable. I braided my hair and wore two scarves over my head, one tied over my forehead and the other tied under my chin. I wore square dark glasses and put on a tight coat. When a Russian approached my berth on the following evening, I pushed my tongue into my lower lip and babbled: "Sick, sick." The Russian laughed and said, "Everybody sick, everybody sick." But he respected my masquerade and I was saved.

Slowly our lives became normal again. Daylight savings time, like they had in Russia, was introduced and the clocks were put forward by two hours. Every evening at ten, hundreds of Russian soldiers assembled at the nearby Oranienplatz and sang their folk songs in the light of the setting sun. I lay in my bed with the window wide open and let myself be sung to sleep. The scent of lime trees invaded the room and a feeling of happiness came over me. Peace. Gone were all those sleepless nights, the rain of bombs, and the gunfire. I hoped I would never experience all of that again.

Weeks later, when our borough of Kreuzberg was given over to the Americans, we became acquainted with other aspects of peacetime — nylon stockings and Camel cigarettes. On the walls of the houses we saw for the first time the words painted: "Ami, go home!"

Born 1937. Handicapped by polio at the age of two. Worked as a salesperson and as a housekeeper. Married. Has three children.

1988

No More Cake Till the War Is Over

I grew up on a small farm in Boeckingen, an old part of Heilbronn. Three generations of our family lived together under one roof. There was a lot of room in the house, a lovely orchard, and a kitchen garden. We even had a farmhand. During the course of the war, foreign workers from France or Russia worked on our farm. There was also for one year a young woman doing her compulsory service. My father had not been mobilized because he was very hard of hearing.

I attended a Christian children's kindergarten where we prayed with the teacher for our Führer and the Fatherland. One day I went to a birthday party with my grandmother. I can still see quite clearly in my imagination the basket full of edibles we brought with us. I was given a plate filled with goodies as a present, which I prized as though it was a great treasure.

The most vivid memory of my first day at school was the flag-raising in the schoolyard and the singing of patriotic songs that I did not know. A classmate explained to me that if I didn't join the *Jungmädel* [young girl's league], I would not be allowed to wear a uniform like the other children and I would not be given a swastika flag to hang outside my window.

When I was six years old, war became a very real fact in my life. In February 1944, a few weeks after my grandfather died, a relative of ours accompanied my parents, myself, my five-year-old sister and our three-year-old brother to the cemetery to visit his grave. While there, our relative took a photo which was to be our last family photo.

On Sunday, September 10, a beautiful day in late summer, there was an air raid. We three children were in an air-raid shelter in the cellar of our neighbor's house. My mother was busy cooking the midday meal, for at that time air raids were not yet taken very seriously. My father, who had been with us up till then, left to see to the cattle, which were mooing quite loudly. A neighbor called out to him: "Richard, stay here, the planes are above us!" But apparently he did not hear. At that moment our mother was in our cellar, where she had gone to fetch some oil. I remember the deafening noise followed by clouds of dust. We children clung close together on the floorboards in the cellar, screaming with fear, "We've been hit!" We were all terrified. It wasn't long before we knew that my father was lying dead in the hayloft, but that my mother had survived without injury. Grandma, frightened but uninjured, came running out of her sitting-room. The Russian farmworker came running toward us from his room under the roof. He was completely unharmed.

It was a scene of horror and the whole place was in a terrible mess. I still see clearly before me the gigantic holes made by the bombs in the middle of the street. The roofs of the house, the stable and the loft had all been torn off. All the windowpanes were broken. The doors were partly ripped from their hinges. A search was made for missing neighbors. Swine stampeded through the yard, sniffing and pawing the dead. The bodies of those who had been killed were laid out in the gymnasium. Long rows of graves were dug in the cemetery. Before the funeral took place our mother went with us to the cemetery, where we saw open graves. When someone drew Mother's attention to the fact that it was not yet known who would be buried where, or just where our father's coffin was in the long row, she replied, "I know exactly where it is." At a certain place, she ordered us children to throw our flowers on the coffin. Her great sorrow was not alleviated by the fact that the Russian farmhand had survived completely uninjured! During the funeral service she fainted, and I often witnessed such fainting spells in the years to come. I worried a great deal about my mother.

After my father's death it seemed like we lived from one alert to the next. It was exhausting and terrifying for my mother, for us children, and especially for my little brother to be awakened abruptly out of sleep every night. I made a fuss, too, because each time we had to go to the air-raid shelter I insisted upon carrying a lantern decorated with a swastika, which somebody had given me as a present.

We were not allowed to have any lights on at night. Cities had to be totally dark, so they could not be spotted by the bombers. On the night of December 4 our city was bombed, and it seemed like everything was ablaze. I watched as muffled figures passed outside. Someone said, "The people who live in these houses will never come out." Once again, many of the inhabitants of Boeckingen were killed. During still another bombing, nearly all the members of a neighboring farm family were killed. They were gathered together at the wedding reception of one of their daughters. Only the bride's sister, who was not in the house at the time, survived.

During another bombing, on January 20, 1945, our house was so badly damaged that we could no longer live there. It was a Saturday, and my mother had just made cake batter that was to be fetched by the baker to bake in his oven. We were not allowed to use our own oven because wood and coal were so scarce. There was another air raid and we had to go to the cellar. On our return we found the cake covered with pieces of broken glass and pieces of mortar. "I will never make another cake until the war is over," my mother said.

During that air raid, our neighbors lost their son Ludwig. He was a carpenter's apprentice in Heilbronn and was on his way home when he was hit by a bomb. Ludwig was the fourth son that this family had lost.

After we were evacuated from our house, we lived in one room a few hundred meters from the stable. We could still use the kitchen, so we were constantly going back and forth. This was a terribly difficult time for my mother. Grandfather had died, father had been killed, and the farmhand had run away. Only one other adult — Grandma — was still alive. She lived in the front part of the house, which had not been entirely destroyed.

Mother had never been taught how to run the farm and she had no experience doing that. Until just a short time before, there had always been at least two men who worked on the farm. We were still living in one room when, in April 1945, the Americans marched in and occupied our town. We had to show our identity cards. My mother, who had none, was packed into a truck and driven off. We children were terribly frightened, but our neighbor comforted us and Mother called out, "I'll be back soon!" Luckily, she was!

To this day I have visions of long rows of prisoners of war as they marched through the streets. Our attempts to give them food were usually thwarted by their guards. Amidst all of the chaos and confusion, many strangers drifted into our lives. I often think of a refugee from the East who assured us that at home she had a beautiful white enamel stove. At that time such a thing seemed like such a luxury.

Losing control of our home to the occupying soldiers was most unpleasant. We were afraid of the soldiers. But it wasn't long before the well which had been destroyed by the bombs was replaced and we moved back into our old house again. I didn't think that there was anything in our old farmhouse that we needed to hide. Years later, when I found a copy of *Mein Kampf* up in the attic, I had to laugh at myself.

I am glad that I was only seven years old at the time. Then I felt as though something new and better was beginning, and I believed that the grown-ups had that feeling too. The sadness over all that had been lost began to disappear. By May, when I was eight years old, I began to think about going to school again. The war was over. Mother could bake a cake again.

BOMBING OF
HEILBRONN

Born in 1931, in Hamburg. During her early childhood spent many nights in air-raid shelters. Worked for fifteen years as a secretary in a publishing company in Heilbronn. Became a pacifist and peace activist. Married. Has three daughters.

A Sunny Autumn Day

The first big air raid on Heilbronn occurred on the morning of September 10, 1944, when I was thirteen years old. It only lasted for six or seven minutes. During that time one hundred B-24 bombers released a shower of explosives and incendiary bombs. Two hundred and eighty people were killed.

My aunt and uncle's house was completely destroyed in a direct hit. They were on their way home from church when the alert took them completely by surprise. When the raid was over they came home to find that their house was a smoking ruin. Under the heavy stones and the smoking beams, seven people who had been in the house were killed. Their little son was dead when they found him. Their daughter, a schoolgirl, was critically injured. My mother visited her in the hospital and came home weeping and completely shaken.

"How is Dorle?" I asked anxiously. "Is she in pain?"

"No," my mother said, "she is not in pain, but she asked me to bring her a hot-water bottle. 'Auntie,' she said, 'will you bring me a hot-water bottle? I have such awfully cold feet. I'm so cold!'"

My mother promised to bring the bottle, but Dorle could not use it to warm her feet. She no longer had any legs. She died on that sunny autumn day.

Born 1912. Worked with the underground resistance during the Nazi era and as an office worker after the war. Retired since 1975. Has one daughter and eight grandchildren.

1942

What Happened To All Those People?

On Monday, December 4, 1944, I had my regular day off to do housework, just like most young working women. On that day I put on my best suit, and my brown velvet hat — I had such an urge to take a walk through town. On November 11, I had visited my Aunt Mina on her birthday and she had said to me: "We're all going to perish here in the city. What did they do with all the Jewish families — with the Sangers — they were such proper people — with the Gummersheimers, the Reis family, the May family and all the others — men who fought in the first war? We'll have to atone for these crimes. Because of that bum (she meant Hitler) we shall perish."

And that's exactly what happened.

I looked in the windows of shops that used to belong to Jews. My heart was heavy when I thought of Dr. Bacharach, the Talheimers, Wurzburgers, Grunefelds, Schwarzs, and the Rosengarts. Were any of these people still alive? And where did they live?

I looked at the old houses in the narrow streets. Past the cinema, the marketplace, the city hall, the Kilian Church. Should I go to the movies or a cafe? Suddenly I was drawn out of the city, past the Brown House [local Nazi party headquarters], to my parents' house. I had hardly entered the apartment when I heard the alarm, the wail of sirens. Mother was just putting supper on the table. Fried potatoes, wurst, beetroot salad. Father was standing at the window and called out: "The Christmas tree flares are already hanging in the sky. They're marking off the area." And to me, less loud: "Today it's our turn."

The first bombs fell. We got into the cellar. The young woman from the second floor was there with her two small children; so were the widow from the first war and her daughter, and the policeman's wife. My mother took her grandson, little Rolf, in her arms. A young mother who was living in the house held her baby tightly — and the bombs fell loudly, exploding as they hit. Through the cellar window we saw fire. We sat motionless and silent. There was a leaden quiet in me. First there had been war in our country, and now it was in our home.

My father went to the cellar steps. The sewer cover in front of the door had been ripped away, and he put boards over it. He said: "The coal in the cellar is already burning. We have to get out of here, behind the house, into the yard."

We saw that the attic was ablaze. No more bombs were falling, but we heard the planes flying back and forth over the burning houses, and the crackle of the fire. How many people were dying now in the cellars, on the street?

You pity us? Who had pity on the Polish, Russian, Czechoslovakian, French and Jewish people? And on those in Leningrad and in the concentration camps?

The next day I thought that I could take my parents to my apartment next to the old cemetery, but we could hardly get through. Everything was razed to the ground. You could see far into the distance, since now there were no buildings to block the view. We had to climb over giant stones, and blackened tree trunks blocked our path. Then we saw the dead burned black lying in a row. The majority were women and children. There were dead mothers with their dead babies pressed to their breasts, and bodies of women still wearing gas masks. A mother with an empty expression pulled a wagon toward the cemetery, with her two dead children, stiff as dolls. This is a picture I shall never forget.

Only a rubbish heap remained where my apartment had been. Written on the one remaining wall were these words: "Wilma, come to Grossgartach!" This gave me a good feeling! People were seeking one another, helping each other. Hate must subside. Love will win! It will be stronger than death and destruction! The war must surely be over soon.

But it lasted one — two — three — four months. A horrible time during which even more people died senselessly — the Nazi fanatics became more brutal as the end neared.

I saw the Americans arrive on April 13, 1945. "The war is over! — *Danke* — *Danke* — *Danke*! I stood alone in the garden next to the house. It was the most beautiful sunshine, the most beautiful springtime. Two planes flew overhead, but I knew no more bombs would be dropped. People could breathe again. I picked some flowers and raised them to the sky. My soul was as if in prayer.

Born 1900. Her husband, a gynecologist who was opposed to the Nazis, was conscripted as an army surgeon. In 1944 he was forced by his superior officers to shoot himself. She was never informed as to the reasons or circumstances of his death. Had three children. Died 1985.

In the Middle of It All

My husband, Dr. Kahleyss, had a small, private clinic for women, with twelve beds. When the war started, he was one of the first doctors in Heilbronn to be drafted, even though he wasn't a surgeon and although he ran a private clinic. But he wasn't a National Socialist and they called up unpopular people first. My husband only had a few hours after receiving mobilization orders to take care of the most urgent business before leaving.

Within days after his departure, the city requested that I lease them the clinic with all its equipment — every bed would be needed soon. Our clinic thus became a municipal maternity ward at the disposal of any doctor for deliveries. There was now only city nursing personnel, Head Nurse Frieda, and a younger nurse. Frieda was a very capable person, considerate, friendly, helpful. She was also a help to me when I had to go into the air-raid shelter with my three children.

The clinic was on the first and second floors. Our apartment was above it on the third floor. From then on the two nurses took all their meals with my family.

On the evening of December 4, 1944, upon hearing the air raid sirens, the nurses took the new mothers down into the cellar as usual. The cellar had a vaulted ceiling, as a winegrower had once lived there, and it was considered bomb-proof. There were two connecting rooms. One was private, for myself and my children; the other was for the clinic patients. There were a few cots in our room so the children could sleep there if need be. In the other room there were some extra benches, because we had to take in people from the street. There was also a barrel of cider which was to prove very valuable.

We had hardly gotten downstairs when there was an unimaginable crash and roar. The clinic was in the center of town. We were in the middle of the attack. One of the last bombs demolished our house. The vault of the basement swayed back and forth. The coal in the cellar next to ours caught fire, and soon the heat was unbearable. We were terribly thirsty. Frieda remembered the cider and we all drank some. I don't know if we would have survived without the juice.

The heavy double iron doors to the shelter were red-hot from the fire. No one could get out that way anymore. We found an iron ladder to use as an exit to the street. All of a sudden someone up there knocked and said, "Is someone still in there? Whoever can still make it out should come up."

My two oldest children went first. I can still see today the way they trembled as they climbed up the ladder. The little one, not yet six, lay unconscious on the floor. I thought she was dead. I wanted to pick her up, but she was too heavy. I cried "Help me!" and a soldier actually came down into the cellar, grabbed the child's hands and dragged her up. I tried to climb out. The soldier grabbed my hands too. That's when I fainted. When I came to I was lying in the front yard and all three children sat around me. I saw the flames shoot up out of the cellar. I heard later that all the clinic women and their newborns had been saved.

I set out with my children to look for shelter. The children had put on only their indoor clothes over their pajamas, and it was December — a cold night. But it was almost hot in town after the firestorm. The sky was amber red and it was very bright. There were bomb craters everywhere, with corpses next to them, some burned to skeletons. Along the whole street everything was burned up.

We wanted to go to a friend's house to see if we could stay with them. When we reached their street we were dismayed to see that there were no houses standing. After wandering around for hours we finally found a place to stay in an overcrowded apartment on the edge of town. Miraculously, the houses there were still standing. The three children fell to the ground sick with exhaustion and anxiety. It was horrible. I had to leave them in their dirty clothes. The woman who had taken us into her house said, "It doesn't make any difference now."

GERTRUD HOFSTETTER

Born 1917. Has been ill ever since the war. Worked in a shoe factory. Married 1939. Husband died in action, 1943. Has two sons.

When I Close My Eyes at Night

There was an alarm on December 4, 1944, at about seven in the evening. The so-called "Christmas tree" flares, announcing an air attack, hung in the sky over the entire city. When I hurried into our cellar with my two small children, I found that others were there already. The first bomb fell as we arrived. Our cellar was so shaken from the attack that six women had to throw their weight against the iron door to keep it from flying open from the blast.

In the meantime our children had crawled into the air-raid cots out of fear. The attack lasted half an hour. After the all-clear signal I noticed that firebombs had fallen into our attic. I managed to throw them out the window before they caused more damage.

The town was ablaze. I wanted to see whether my friends were still alive. That's why I set out through the sea of flames. I left my two children in the care of an older couple. Flames leaped up at me from all the bomb craters. I walked away from our home on the sidewalks (the tarred streets were on fire) and heard ghastly cries from the air-raid shelters. The air-raid wardens were under orders to keep the doors closed, even though people in the cellars were suffocating.

Crouched together in the front yard of Dr. Kahleyss's clinic were small children and a mother with her newborn baby. Everything was in flames. I was seized by a feeling of horror. I could no longer stand the sight of the many dead, and went home to my children.

The ones who had stayed at home were in great despair. A woman who had had a child a few weeks before the attack had gone mad. Shortly before the raid she had learned that her husband had been killed in action. She couldn't cope with so much misfortune and was no longer able to care for her child.

It was winter, all the windowpanes in our building were broken by the blasts, making the house temporarily uninhabitable. That night everyone who had found refuge in our basement walked up to the artillery barracks. As wives of soldiers, in my case a widow, we had the right to shelter in the barracks.

I had taken charge of the neglected child and placed him in the baby carriage with my own children. I could only pack a little clothing, and a baby bottle for the children. I had to make my way with the carriage around numerous bomb craters in some of which lay whole sections of houses. The walk through the cold winter night seemed endless.

When we arrived in the barracks we were given air-raid bunks and milk for the children. I tried to warm the milk a little over a candle flame. We stayed there for about eight days. By then the soldiers had hammered boards across the windows in our house.

The barracks stood on a hill and we could watch with binoculars as the dead were brought to the mass grave in wheelbarrows and trucks. They were thrown into giant holes. Men in white coats threw lime over the bodies after each load: a layer of lime, a layer of people, lime, people, lime, people . . . it went on for days.

To this day when I close my eyes at night I see the dead in the lime pit. I will never be able to forget them.

Born in the early 1900s. Learned of this book project through a local newspaper and mailed her story to the peace group in 1985. Lived at that time in a nursing home.

His Hair Turned White

*A*n event like the bombing of Heilbronn on December 4, 1944, can only be described by someone who witnessed the catastrophe. The whistling and crash of the bombs, the fear — is the next one for us? Even now, forty years later, I shudder when someone speaks of it.

The morning after the bombing the smoke and the smell of burning flesh — people and animals — hung over the city of ruins. Russian prisoners of war had to find the bodies amidst the rubble in the cellars and haul them to waiting trucks. This task was extremely dangerous because of the mines and unexploded ammunition which lay all about. Relatives of those who had died would often struggle against the authorities to take possession of the bodies of their loved ones.

My son was ten years old at the time. After the attack, we squeezed out of the cellar on hands and knees through the ruins of our house. The next morning my son had snow-white hair on the back of his head. He still has it today. When he was twenty years old, he said that all of his dreams at night still revolved around this horrible attack.

Born 1923. Served as a soldier in the German army and was on duty December 4, 1944, during the air raid on Heilbronn. Married 1945. Has five children and five grandchildren.

1941

The Day After

T he horrible night of the air attack on Heilbronn was over. Then began the terrifying search for relatives. We were half choking on smoke and our clothes were scorched.

On the morning of December 5, I continued the search for my in-laws, my eyes watering, coughing painfully from the firestorm the night before, and hoping that they had somehow been able to survive the fire. On that morning, full of horror, we could first comprehend the devastating effect of the night attack. What we had taken for burning timbers and trees the night before were bodies, burned beyond recognition, now lying on the street between houses that were split open and still burning. On my way I passed Kaiser

Wilhelmplatz, where the pointed steeple of the Peace Church, burned black, was still standing. There was a women's clinic nearby. The recovered bodies lay next to the ruins: young mothers, infants, a few days old or newborn, maybe a premature birth during the horrors of the night, killed immediately. I was twenty-one years old. I was so horrified at the senseless death of these innocent children that I still remember the sight of the bodies. Sometimes it troubles me in my dreams even today — forty years later.

Back then, at the sight of that misery, I made up my mind that if I survived the war — which was to rage over our country for six more months — I would do everything in my power to preserve peace, and to make clear at every possible opportunity that war, for whatever reason it might be waged, is wrong.

[In the beginning of the war most Germans, although they knew that the Jews were being taken to "work camps," did not realize that they were being killed. It was thought that the Jews were merely being forced to do heavy labor. Toward the end of the war young German soldiers were ordered to duty inside the concentration camps. This duty was so horrific that some of the soldiers committed suicide rather than carry out the orders. Hints of what was going on inside the concentration camps spread across the country.]

Born 1919. Worked in the post office. Now retired. Married 1943. Son born March 1944 and died September 1944. Two daughters born after the war. Four grandchildren.

1946

I'll Find Mama for You

I was on the late shift on December 4, 1944. Around seven in the evening the sirens started, even in Bönnigheim, where I was working. We had hardly reached the cellar when my boss called me back upstairs: "It's Heilbronn today." We stood there and looked into the Neckar Valley and at the silhouette of Heilbronn, brightly illuminated by the "Christmas tree" flares. We saw the glare of blazing red fire over the city, the air battles above — we saw one plane going into a tailspin. It looked as if it was coming right at us, but then it crashed not far away in a field. I can't explain it, but from where we stood you normally couldn't see anything. I went back often afterwards. You really can't see anything. But on that night we saw the path of the Neckar, every village, and the sea of flames above Heil-bronn as clearly as on a map.

Many people living in less solid houses in the southern district of Heilbronn spent the nights in deep cellars. My father and step-mother had rented a place to sleep in one of these cellars downtown. Underground passages were made between the big cellars and then blocked off again. In an emergency you could break through to get from one cellar to another. That night it was bearable in the cellar where my parents were. But then the people from the neighboring cellar were in trouble and broke through the passage. With the people came smoke. Air was limited. The air-raid warden who stood guard in a uniform with a pistol warned: "Whoever leaves will be shot."

When they could hardly breathe anymore, he sent a few men up to see if everyone could leave. My father was the first to go out. He said to Mama: "I'll wait for you at the Robert Mayer Memorial." My father crawled out the emergency exit, burning both hands when he touched the ground. He had put them down onto burning asphalt or phosphorous. He also had serious burns on his neck. He dragged himself to the memorial. He sat there and waited and waited and could not be convinced to move from the spot. In the end some people took him to the barracks where the wounded were ban-daged. After he was bandaged and given eyedrops so that he could see again, he dragged himself home.

The next morning I rode home on my bike. Bönnigheim didn't have a train station, so I always traveled the fifteen kilometers to Heilbronn by bicycle. Outside of Heilbronn I was stopped by a sen-try and asked where I was going. "To my parents in the southern district," I said. He let me go. Nothing much had happened to our house. My father had left a note: "I'm at my brother's." I found my father at my uncle's. There was no sign of Mama. "I think Mama is dead," my father said. I went off to look for her but I didn't get very far. No one could enter the downtown area. I asked at the barracks but no one knew anything. In the evening my father and I tried to get downtown by bike. A fire truck took us part of the way. The trip was a terrible strain for my father because of his injuries.

The next day I rode downtown again. "I'll find Mama for you," I had promised my father. I was told that many of the dead were laid out on the main street to be identified. I climbed over ruins to get to the main street.

The first bodies I came to looked like charred branches, like a piece of tree trunk, totally black. Many of the dead were already covered over. Since I knew Mama's shoes I thought I wouldn't have to take off the blankets all the way; it would be enough just to see the shoes. But many legs and feet were burned off, so I had to look closer. Since I couldn't find my stepmother on the main street, I looked in the hall run by the civil defense. There were many dead there, too. Then I went down a very long street which was lined by bodies on each side. I looked at them all — I went also into the air-raid shelter — but I couldn't find her. It was noon in the meantime and I couldn't continue. I went to a friend, who is now my sister-in-law. When she saw what shape I was in, she told me to wait in the house and she went out to look for my mother. She found my stepmother relatively quickly, in a building not far from her home. Now I had to go there and identify the body. Mama looked as if she were sleeping peacefully. She had fainted from lack of oxygen. She was wearing a thick belt. That's probably how they lifted her out of the cellar. My father later learned that she was still alive when they rescued her. She was supposed to be given an oxygen mask, but it was too late.

The men from the civil defense had to remove her wedding ring and wristwatch with pliers because rigor mortis had set in. After that I had to notify the registration office of her death. From there they sent me back to tie a tag with personal data on my stepmother's foot. After I had completed all of this, night had fallen and I got on my bike to ride home. I got a flat tire on the way which couldn't be repaired. So I had to walk. I arrived late at night. Without a word I placed the severed-off ring and wristwatch on the table in front of my father. He knew.

NEARING THE END

Born 1930. An office worker currently employed by an insurance company. A member of the Green Party. Divorced. Has three daughters.

1943

1987

Shopping Trip

*I*was fourteen years old. It was the beginning of March 1945, a clear, sunny day. My mother sent me to town to do some shopping, a not unusual occurrence — but this shopping trip would be engraved on my memory forever.

We lived in a cottage in a vineyard outside Boeckingen. We had run out of sugar, salt, bread and many other staples several days earlier. But every time my mother tried to send me to town there was a bombing alert and I couldn't leave. Now we could put off the shopping no longer. It was thus with a heavy heart that my mother sent me off with a long shopping list and the food ration stamps.

Shortly before I reached the edge of town, the first fighter planes rushed over me in the sky. Before they were able to spot me, I ducked for cover on a ridge of the vineyard. I couldn't move and had to keep very still until the planes were out of sight, since they shot at everything that moved. I waited until I no longer heard the sound of the planes before I continued on my way. My joy at not having been discovered by the fighter planes was premature. When I reached a residential area and was walking beside the high garden walls, once again I heard the sound of motors. I could tell by the high whistling sound that the planes were coming in for a new attack. I quickly pressed myself into a garden gate entrance. At that very moment the machine-gunners on board the planes rattled off their rounds of ammunition. Although I could feel the bullets all around me I was not hit. I had escaped once again.

Unscathed, I reached the dairy store in Sontheimerstrasse, which also carried other groceries and bread. I waited to be served (there were no self-service shops in those days). Just as the shop-keeper and I finished packing my bags, we heard the sound of sirens — an air-raid warning, first alarm stage. I wanted to rush from the shop and head back to the vineyards. I figured that I could make it home by the time the main alarm sounded. But the couple who owned the shop would not permit me to leave. They forced me and several other customers into the cellar of the house.

The sirens sounded again — acute danger! When I got into the cellar, I looked around. In the course of the years of war I had learned about the requirements for a bomb shelter; the one in which I now found myself did not meet them. I asked the owner of the house where the emergency exit for this cellar was located. He said there was none. I also noticed that this cellar had a flat ceiling. Previous bombing attacks had revealed that cellars with flat ceilings collapsed more easily, burying the people under them. I told the owner of the house, who apparently felt responsible for me, that I would, under no circumstances, stay there.

In the meantime we could hear the enemy planes, whose rumbling engines made the house tremble. But even that could not stop me from leaving that cellar and that house.

I had to pause for a moment at the door of the house, because the sunlight was blinding after the semi-darkness of the cellar. Then I proceeded along the wall of the house until I heard a man's voice asking me what I was doing. I looked up into the face of a German soldier. He looked friendlier than his voice had sounded. He and another soldier were leaning on the wall of the neighboring house. When I told them why I had left the so-called shelter, they under-stood; they too had refused a similar shelter. And then the low-flying planes roared over us and I felt weak in my stomach! One of the soldiers screamed "Get down!" and pushed me from the wall to the ground.

There would be a short breathing period before the next attack wave approached. In the interval I asked the soldiers whether they knew what the bombing target was. They said it was directed against the main train station and the freight yard in Boeckingen, to prevent further supply shipments.

The attack lasted about twenty minutes. The two soldiers didn't seem to be bothered by it. I thought to myself that they had probably already experienced far worse things at the front.

It wasn't until then that I noticed how I was shaking all over, I was so terribly afraid. I thought of my mother in our house at the edge of the woods, and the fear she must be feeling for me as she watched the planes diving in the direction of the town, dropping their bombs.

Didn't those men sitting in the fighter planes and bombers know that women and children have souls and hearts and must withstand horrible fear during such terrible attacks?

The soldier at my side nudged me — all clear! I said goodbye to both of them and thanked them for taking care of me. As quickly as possible — half running, half walking — I hurried up the hill with my heavy bags, listening for sounds above me. Sometimes I had to stop and catch my breath. But the fear I had just experienced and my anxiety about what might yet come drove me up the mountain. I didn't feel safe until my mother took me in her arms without a word. Tears poured down her cheeks.

Born 1919. Worked during the war as a forced laborer in the arms industry. Lost several members of her family in air raids. Married 1943. Has one daughter and two granddaughters.

1943

1985

You Can Go On

After our house was bombed, we were assigned to a small room in the Rose Inn at Neckarsach, just near Heilbronn. There was a concentration camp nearby, and the men — mostly Poles and Russians, with grey-and-blue-striped uniforms and caps — were put to work in various places around Neckarsach. Every morning some of them were driven past the inn in a truck. They stood in the truck, holding onto each other. We felt so sorry for them!

We started to save some of our bread for them, figuring that they must be even hungrier than we were. And Mother and I always stood at the window when the truck came by. We were happy at those times when we succeeded in throwing some of the bread to the men at just the right moment. Even though we knew it was forbidden, we did it again and again.

Another group from the concentration camp marched by the inn on the way to work every day. Often two men had to carry one of their comrades between them because he could hardly walk. And it often happened that one comrade had to take another comrade back to the camp in a wheelbarrow. How tired and weak they were? It was a horrible sight, day after day.

Once while out for a walk, I came to the Ship Inn, which formerly had been a dance hall but now was used to store sacks of cement. It was the job of the men from the concentration camp to load these sacks onto trucks. At the entrance an armed soldier stood guard. I recognized him; he was often a guest in the inn in the evenings. An older man with a sack on his back had to go down a few steps which led outside. He seemed to be at the end of his strength. The soldier gave this ill-treated man a kick and said to him: "You see, you can go on!" I was horrified at so much inhumanity and brutality, but I couldn't do anything about it. I could only think that tomorrow there would be one less man who would be able to work.

That same evening I sat with my husband in the restaurant of the inn, listening to the radio. Also sitting at our table was the soldier I had seen at the cement-loading place that afternoon. I asked him: "Why did you do that today? That man you kicked was certainly a man with a family. I saw what you did. His harsh response to this was, "If you don't keep your mouth shut, you know what will happen to you!"

[Gertrud Pietsch wrote the letters that follow to Erhart Kaest-
ner who later became a famous writer. In 1945 he wrote *Zeit-
buch von Tumilat* about his experience as a prisoner of war in
Egypt. Pietsch wrote these letters from the hills above Dresden, where streams of refugees from Czechoslovakia were
moving west to flee the Russian army.]

Letters To a Prisoner of War

February 1945

Dear Erhart,

The contents of this letter are probably the most difficult of any
I have ever written to you. It takes so much strength even to be half-
way able to write to you. And the tears keep pouring from my eyes.
Our grief overwhelms us and the worry about what will come.

On the thirteenth of February I stood on the summit of Alten-
berg in the Erzgebirge [Ore Mountains] and stared at the burning
sea below — the destruction of Dresden. It was like a giant, glowing
ball. Our beloved Dresden. And I knew of parents, siblings and
friends who were there. We all held each others' hands, complete

strangers. I thought I would surely die.

Early on the nineteenth, the stars were still shining and God was in Heaven above me. I went with my lantern to a bright, good house, prayed for strength and gave birth to my son in the morning. A life in my arms, sent in these days of annihilation! On the fourth day, I got up. One of my brothers had arrived. He had looked in vain for our parents in Dresden. Our poor mother's body was found in a burned-out house, sunk behind the door, very tiny. We will never know how or where our father died. In the meantime a steady stream of friends and acquaintances came up from the burned-out city to our mountain. More and more people, a stream which even today has not run dry. I am surrounded by people I know and people I don't know and by a host of children, and none of them have anything, not even the most essential things. I shared what I could.

There was no opportunity to rest. Nevertheless I am regaining my strength. I sit here nursing my child among the many who are crying, and I don't know where to begin.

In the midst of all this misery a reading-evening was held last night: *Hermann and Dorothea*! It was touching — the banished, the people who had come together from all over, cooped up in a small room. "Death is not a shock to the wise and it is not the end for the pious."

I often go out in the evening to look at the stars . . .

March 1945

Dear Erhart,

For weeks refugees had been coming across the Czechoslovakian border, over the mountain ridge near Zinnwald. During the day there were mostly old people, the handicapped, children, women with baby carriages. Our community took in mothers with babies. We constantly kept warm water on the stove for a quick bath. They couldn't stay long; they were always fearful of missing their connection — to where, no one knew.

I quickly made some porridge for the child of a desperate young mother who could no longer nurse it, as a result of the strain and excitement. I made it very thin so that the baby would be able to swallow it. After much patience on its mother's part, the baby finally swallowed it! The mother cried for joy, and we cried with her! Her child had been born the same month as my small son. I gave her some of my supplies for the journey. But she didn't want to take charity from anyone, so in exchange she gave me a bag of black tea which she had been able to save. What odd things the refugees often carried with them — things they had grabbed in desperation at the last minute. But it was just this tea which was to save us. The worry of having three small children to feed every day, of trying to give them as much food as possible and to help them over sickness — this worry was always with us. My small son had grown very weak because of constant diarrhea. Our doctor had no medicine for him. "If you only had some black tea!" And now we had this miracle tea and it really did help. Blessed be that young refugee woman! Later a letter from her arrived from Thüringen — the child survived.

Born 1941. Student of theology and interested in social, ecological and political issues. A peace activist and the owner of a health food store. Married. Has three daughters.

1948

Gold Buttons

I was born in August 1941. Memories of my childhood and the war are a part of me. Mostly only those of the older generation talk about the war. Why do the people of my generation remain silent?

I believe that we "war children" have not been asked enough about our experience. Much has been forgotten, deliberately — the war years of our youth, the years of reconstruction after the war, which was a time of modest optimism. The reality of our experience as children contradicted how we wished it might have been. Nobody wanted to remember how innocent little children had suffered from destruction, wounds, separation and death. We would like to pretend that there was some security, not dying parents. How often, in later years, did I hear the artless phrase: "You must remember something of the war years." With time the wish to forget was fulfilled. The memories seem to have vanished although the fear, uncertainty, nightmares and illness remain. Ordinary connections were forgotten. And yet it is clear that although forty years have passed, the psychology and the life history of our generation which, began in war was shaped by that war.

Only after intense probing through psychoanalysis was I able to begin to recall the past and reconstruct my relationship with my parents.

We children lived with my parents in Sulau, a very small town in Silesia, near the Polish border. My father who had been drafted was at the front. My brother and I were conceived while he was home on leave. The few photos I have of him were taken while he was home on short furloughs. I remember once when my father arrived without warning. I was walking in the woods with my mother when suddenly my father came laughing and walking toward us from another path. When I think of that event I can still see my mother's joy. On the other hand, the feeling I have about her sadness and her anxiety for him when he returned to the front is just as intense.

In September 1944, when I was three years old, news arrived of my father's death. My brother and I were called in from the sandbox where we were playing. We came into father's study. My mother, my aunt and my elder sister were weeping bitterly. It was all too much for me. I did not want their sadness. I was especially embarrassed by my sister's weeping. I remember very distinctly my thoughts at that time. Why cry over father's death? He was very seldom here, not at all important for us! Nevertheless I continued to ponder his death for a long time. My brother who is a year older than I comforted me by saying, "We can still write to Father where he is now, in heaven. We'll have to use an envelope with a black border." For a long time Papa came back to me from time to time in dreams. He looked radiant, like he used to look when on a long walk. Nevertheless, I was afraid of him because he was rather like that other Father in Heaven; like God, surpassing all, infinitely kind, but terribly inflexible.

My real world was full of women, with my mother being the focal point. She was strong and competent, yet soft and kind as she went around supervising everything. My feelings and thoughts were completely determined by her. My mother was left in charge of the Protestant parish of which my father had been the minister before he was drafted. She was kept very busy with her work and with the family. As children of the minister my sister and brothers and myself all held a prominent position in the community.

As far back as I can remember we were trained to understand that anything spoken or discussed at home was never to be mentioned outside the house. I knew there was a very good reason for us to keep secrets. If we told a secret we could be in acute danger.

Often after dark a young Polish woman, Julia, would visit our house. I have a blurred recollection of Julia as a kind woman who was a forced laborer. She and my mother were friends although it was strictly forbidden for them to meet. I don't know if I ever questioned why this was. As far back as I can remember I have known the word "Nazi" with its dangerous tone. I knew the words "Jew" and "Pole." I knew that it was dangerous to think of them as friends. The knowledge that my mother knew more than I and more than other people seemed both dangerous and soothing.

At night we slept in a darkened room. My mother kept a radio hidden under a woolen blanket and would listen to foreign stations. We listened also to the sound of footsteps outside the house. It was such a relief when they passed by and died out.

Long before we fled from Silesia my mother knew that we would have to leave. She learned the route across the Oder and the Elbe rivers. From this came my first notion of geography. The weather was cold and snowy and I was not allowed to go outside because I had been ill. Sometimes when I stood on a small stool at the window and looked down on the street at men constructing a makeshift wall which divided the town, Mother would stand behind me and watch too. When I asked her why they were building a wall she laughed and said scornfully, "They are building a wall so that the Russians can't pass!" Relieved that this was funny, I laughed with her.

Then we were officially ordered to leave Sulau. My mother began to pack for the trip to Hamburg where my grandmother lived. Mother made big labels with our names and our grandmother's address and sewed them to our clothing. We wore three layers of clothes and carried small knapsacks on our backs. We were allowed to take one doll. We were given a horse-cart to share with another family and there was even a driver who had gold buttons on his thick blue coat. Mother and our aunt placed all the featherbeds and mattresses from the house in the cart so it would be soft, warm and cozy. That pleased me at once! The neighbors lamented, "That good bedding on the horse-cart!" My mother knew the war was lost and we would not be coming back, so the featherbeds were fulfilling a last good purpose. I do not know if she dared say that to the neighbors. We were not allowed to admit that the war was lost.

We traveled for seven days through the wintry countryside. Endless caravans of horse-carts traveled down roads with snow piled high on both sides. At the crossroads one met with more caravans coming from another direction. Travel was slow — very slow. The voices of the adults were filled with panic. "Max, hold the horses tight, or we'll all fall in the ditch!" I can still hear my mother call out to the coachman who had almost fallen asleep: "Cross the Oder before the bridge is blown up!" I remember that sentence as one remembers a nursery rhyme. Men in uniform directed traffic at the crossings. They stopped some of the carts and let others go on. We were lucky and were allowed to pass quickly. As we crossed the bridge the indescribable relief of the grown-ups was even stronger than the fear which preceded it.

En route we slept in schools and gymnasiums. Big beds of straw, big rooms, screaming babies, lots of strangers, grumbling and lamenting. Before going to sleep Mother would hide her watch and her golden ring. I was happy lying between my mother and my aunt.

In the morning we would climb up on the cart again. My mother arranged everything so that nobody got lost and everything ran smoothly. First the other family would climb into the cart, then my elder sister and brother followed by my mother carrying my eighteen-month-old brother. Then my aunt climbed into the cart ahead of me so that she could lift me up. Each time before she lifted me, I stood for a few endless seconds alone on the road between strangers, carts and soldiers. What would happen if the horses suddenly moved on and the cart rolled ahead — the whole caravan could roll on past without me? In those few seconds I experienced the greatest anxiety in my life. Although terrified, during the whole flight I never complained, cried or clung to my mother. I did not believe that I, as a small child, was entitled to be especially spared from fear and terror. This experience did not even seem to me to be worthy of any special attention. It was only much later on that I spoke of it within my family.

Once in the cart, the journey itself was comforting. I was happy to lie there amidst the soft warm blankets and let myself be carried along. Most of all I liked the snowy air and the dark evening sky. Our journey lasted for one week. Today I can easily make the same trip by car in two hours. When we arrived in Hamburg there were many relatives to meet us and much confusion. Mother and Grandmother fell into each other's arms and shed tears of joy. I too was happy, but it was all a bit embarrassing.

I have often wondered what happened to the horse-carts and the coachman Max with the golden buttons. Did all the other crowds of people have a grandmother on the other side of the Elbe too?

We lived for two years in my grandmother's house in the country. My memory is crowded with visions of women and small children in that house. The men were all either dead or in prison camps. Women struggled bravely for every pound of potatoes they could muster. They fought each other for the best morsel of food — always for their children.

Grandma had a garden, a sheep and a few hens. Now and then each one of us in turn got an egg — sometimes an extra one for a birthday or another special occasion. Mother whisked the egg white into meringue and managed to sweeten it somehow. Wonderful! But apart from that we were often hungry. Even today I cannot bear the feeling of hunger.

The war was nearing an end. The grown-ups no longer spoke about it in whispers as they had before. But they were still careful. Someone from the village, a man I knew only slightly, hung himself. The reason had something to do with the end of the war. The old Nazis seemed now to be in danger themselves. I couldn't quite understand why that was.

One morning my great-aunt woke us up. "It is peace," she said, but she had a pathetic look on her face. My first happy thought was: "Now it's going to be like it was in the old days when there were oranges and lemons and people could travel." How often had I heard about such lovely things from the grown-ups. Then my aunt said, "We must go to meet the English soldiers outside the village. We must surrender. The adults must carry white towels with them, and the children white handkerchiefs." "Surrender. What does that mean?" No matter, the white handkerchiefs sounded interesting. But Mother came in and explained that because the English soldiers had already arrived in the village, it would not be necessary to surrender. Tanks were being driven over the lovely red streets of the village, destroying them. The village looked desolate, and it hurt our feet when we walked barefoot on the broken bricks.

For a very long while peacetime did not seem so very different than wartime. We still went hungry and still had no house of our own. When we finally did get a house it had no toilet and no running water. Filled with panic and fear at the sight of uniformed soldiers, I tried to persuade my grandmother to hide when military vehicles came into sight. For years I avoided going down a street where there was a military service station. My mother was very weary after the war. Although despondent herself, she tried bravely to encourage us children to go on living.

Born 1920. Worked as salesperson in a butcher shop during the war. Married. Had two sons, one of whom died in infancy. Divorced. Remarried. One daughter.

Always Alone

*T*he Third Reich began for me with a conversation between my uncle and my aunt. My uncle was a railroad supervisor. He asked my aunt: "Emmi, do you have material for a flag in the house? You've got to sew a swastika flag right away. It must be hoisted immediately!" At that time, 1933, I was thirteen years old. I was a member of the youth group of the Stahlhelm [Steel Helmet], called "Little Cornflowers." Soon we were transferred into the National Socialist Youth Organization. That is how I joined the *Jungmädchen* [Young Girls].

I enjoyed going to the meetings. The leader knew how to stimulate our enthusiasm. Of course, soon we were singing patriotic songs and participating in political rallies. But for us this was simply a youth group like the Scouts. Two occurrences from these early years are still very fresh in my mind. One was the rounding up of the communists. The father of one of my classmates was among those arrested. They hung a sign around his neck which said, "I am a traitor to my people." The second incident was the book-burning in our town. We were told to be at the town square at a certain time, but were not told why. All of a sudden, there was a group of SA men [Storm troopers]. We had to stand in formation. The whole town square was full of people in uniform. Books were brought out from a nearby bookstore by the basketful; they had been collected beforehand and were now thrown into a pile and set on fire. We were told this was filthy literature which had to be destroyed.

Nevertheless, the positive experiences by far outweighed the negative ones. The mass meetings with their big marches kindled my enthusiasm. All those uniforms, the members of the guilds in their special clothes, the pennants, the marching music . . . and how proud I was of being permitted to carry a small flag — only blondes were privileged to do that.

When I finished grade school in 1935 it was difficult to find an apprentice position. My father was unemployed, so it was important that I become self-supporting. My mother's sisters finally found an apprenticeship for me in a big butcher shop in Baden-Baden. I was not at all interested in that trade, but under these economically difficult circumstances I had to take the job. I received free lodging and meals. For the first year I received seven marks spending money per month.

In Baden-Baden I joined the *Bund Deutschen Mädchen* [League of German Girls]. The meetings, called "home evenings," were always organized in such a way that we really had fun. There was always a specific program. First, there was the political part in which the leader would talk about a current or historical theme. Then we played games, folk danced or sang. When one of Hitler's speeches was announced, Hitler Youth (boys) and *Bund Deutschen Mädchen* (girls) stood in formation and listened in front of the theatre, where big loudspeakers had been installed. The idea not to take part never occurred to us. We simply went to these meetings. Anyway, "service" in the youth groups was considered of paramount importance. I found out very soon how much power these party organizations could wield.

My supervisor at the butcher shop came from Alsace-Lorraine and she could not identify in any way with these National Socialist meetings. I lived in my employer's house but did not get a house key, so they had to stay up until I came home from an evening meeting. The meetings were usually over by 10:00 P.M. and I could have easily been home at about 10:15 P.M., but we always liked to stay awhile longer and talk, so my supervisor had to wait up late for me. She always complained about this. I finally told the *Bund Deutschen Mädchen* about my supervisor's complaints, and a short while later my employer received an official letter. My supervisor never bothered me again.

Still strong in my memory is a midsummernight's meeting in Baden-Baden. It was an especially festive evening. We climbed silently up a mountain where a great fire had been lit. Once there we sang songs with lyrics like: "Rise, flame, with a great shine from the mountains above the Rhine." We looked far across the Rhine over into France. When the fire burned down we jumped across it in pairs. Everyone had a wonderful time and we did not pay attention to the political aspects of the meeting.

When World War II began, on September 1, 1939, I was in Altenburg, just near the Czech border. All the employees were gathered around a loudspeaker. I saw fear and apprehension in the faces of the older people as they listened to Hitler's speech. We young people did not know what all this meant and we thought that the war would not last long. I knew about war only from what my father, who had fought in the first world war, had told us. His stories seemed to me, as a child, to be about the remote past.

Nothing much changed in my life with the start of the war except that food ration cards caused us a lot of extra work in the butcher shop, where we collected them in a special box. Every evening the coupons we had collected that day were pasted onto large, pre-printed sheets of paper which then had to be sent in and exchanged for new stock. Every evening we sat and pasted these coupons for at least an hour.

At first the rations were generous and there was plenty to buy. Little by little commodities became more scarce, and from about 1942 on there were long lines in front of the various stores. Meanwhile I had married and moved to Berlin. There, too, people stood in line for food, even for the so-called homemade blood and liver sausages which one could get for just "half" ration coupons. This sausage contained anything but meat; mostly it consisted of blood, cream of wheat and barley. At least the women had something to take home to their kitchens.

In the early war years we believed Göring's word that no enemy airplane would ever penetrate as far into Germany as Berlin. When the first heavy bombings came in 1941 the mood all of a sudden was very different. At night we maintained strict blackout by putting black paper in front of the windows. Air raid wardens checked to see that no glimmer of light could be seen. No street lights were lit. In total darkness we hurried through the streets, often bumping into other people. The streetcars had just one tiny light and one could barely see them. On the Kurfürstendamm and a few other main streets curbs were marked with glowing paint, but all side streets were totally dark.

In the spring of 1943 the bombings got worse and worse. My husband was in Russia and I was pregnant, so I returned to southern Germany. When my son was nine months old my husband came back home. He had been sick and had lost all his teeth. He brought me and our child back to Berlin.

In the summer of 1944 we experienced a terrible air attack. The bunker we were in swayed and shook. Everyone looked at the ceiling wondering, "Will it hold or not? Have we been hit?" I wanted to leave Berlin with or without my husband, and made my way through the smoking rubble to the railroad station. There I found a westward-bound train but it was totally filled — people were even hanging on the outside. No one asked where the train was going — everyone just wanted to get away — away from this hell! Somebody pushed me and my child through a train window. Inside the train people were crowded right into the restrooms. Occasionally someone would let me sit on a suitcase or a pack for a few minutes. It took one full day to get to Heilbronn.

My second son was born in the hospital in Eppingen, shortly before the big air attack on Heilbronn. This hospital actually was a women's hospital and so I had a small room for myself heated by a small coal stove. The nurse had just put some water on the stove to heat for the baby's bath when the air-raid sirens screamed. By the time the water was warm the first wounded were brought in from the attack on Heilbronn and the nurse was called into the operating room. I could not get up and the bath water got cold. After about an hour the nurse came back, took the baby and bathed him in the water which had been standing there all this time.

I noticed that something wasn't right with my baby, and I said to the doctor, "This child does not nurse properly; something is wrong." The doctor quickly looked at the baby and said, "Why, he is fit as a fiddle!" and I was released from the hospital. At home, things got worse. The little one could hardly breathe. He had a fever and soon could not take in any nourishment. Once a week a doctor came to the village on a bicycle. He took one hurried look at the baby, did not even listen to his heartbeat or examine him in any way, and said, "A slight cold, nothing more." Two days later my little son died. When we buried the child and stood by the open grave, the enemy planes flew over us in circles and every so often came in very low. I thought, "Soon, very soon, I will be lying beside you, my child," but they did not attack and finally left.

Meanwhile my older son got sick, too. His ears hurt and he cried so much. The village doctor could not help him. I finally took him to Eppingen to another doctor. This doctor immediately sent us to a clinic in Heidelberg. It was a real adventure in the year 1945 to travel from our village to Heidelberg. There were hardly any trains, no private cars, and taxis could only drive when one had a gasoline ration coupon — something even a mother with a sick child could not easily obtain. With all of this and despite not being allowed to travel during daytime hours because of the low-flying enemy planes, we made it! Relatives who owned a service station helped out with gasoline. I was not allowed to stay with my son and had to leave him there in these unsafe times! The second time I came to visit him, my child had disappeared. I had already lost one son — and now this one. "What has happened to him?" I cried out in great fear. I was told they had moved him to the department for contagious diseases because he was sick with diphtheria, and I was not allowed to visit him anymore. I could only look at him through a glass window. The little one cried out, "Mama, Mama," and I had to stay outside and could not go in to him.

I visited my son as often as possible. Time and again I managed somehow to get there — by trains with no windows at five in the morning, by truck, or hitchhiking. Whichever way, I always took a quick look at the sky for enemy attack planes. One time I walked the twenty-five kilometers to the clinic. I was only skin and bones.

Shortly before the arrival of the Americans I was allowed to bring my little boy home. For quite awhile he had a draining wound behind the ear. I always had to clean it with oil — if and when I could get oil — to keep it from getting sticky, and I had to cover it with a thick layer of medicinal cotton.

Meanwhile my husband had been transferred to Italy where he was captured by the Americans and taken to America. For quite awhile he did not know anything of what had happened here at home.

The front line came closer and we spent night and day in the basement. My grandmother gave us a small stove so I could at least warm some milk. As the German troops passed by, this defeated army was an awful sight. Some soldiers walked leaning on sticks, some had their feet wrapped in rags. Totally spent and tired, they moved east. It was said that they were to reorganize once more.

One evening I walked to a nearby farm to ask for some milk. I did not have anything to feed my child. All of a sudden the German soldiers started to open fire. American forces were very close and I was in between the two armies. Bullets whistled above me and I threw myself on the ground. A grenade hit the farm. Still, I could not return to my child without bringing some nourishment. In spite of the shooting, I ran across the farmyard. What else could I do? The child was hungry!

Everything revolved around obtaining food. Even after the Americans came and the war was finally over, this daily hunting for food did not get any easier for a long time. One did almost anything to get something to eat. In the summer we went to the rye fields after they had been harvested to gather spilled grain. Large groups of people would stand by the edge of the field waiting for the farmer to allow them to enter the field. Then everyone rushed forward to find every little kernel of grain which might have fallen to the ground during harvest. Similarly we gathered potatoes left in the field when fall came. Sometimes we found small pieces of corn cobs in the harvested corn fields. We ground up the kernels in our coffee mill and cooked some sort of hot cereal from them. There was scarcely any fat to use in cooking, so when we did not have any we simply cooked with water.

When my husband returned from America we were almost like strangers to each other. After the long time apart we simply could not find a way to get together again. I had grown up a lot during these years, and had become more independent. We had only lived together about half a year after we were married. Maybe our marriage had been something like a "hunger for living" during those early war years. At each parting we never knew whether we would ever see each other again. Many marriages were entered into hastily under these circumstances.

Life in America had been so easy for my husband! He had no idea of the misery we had to go through. When he saw how hungry we were and how hard we worked for a bare existence, and when he heard that our child had died, he could not find any words of sympathy. He only said, "If I had only stayed in America!" There wasn't any togetherness between us anymore and we finally got a divorce.

Looking back, I must say that the influence of National Socialism on my basic attitude has been quite strong. For instance, the teachings about human races [*Rassenlehre*] made a lasting impression on me. I am still of the opinion that it cannot be good to mix up various races. And the big marching formations, the mass meetings, the marching music — I still have a weak spot for all that even to this day. But I know what war is like — and I want peace.

I am frightened by the depot for Pershing II rockets in the forest near Heilbronn. I don't want such terrible weapons to be made ready again, and I don't want anyone in this world to be endangered by such weapons. With all my heart I want disarmament. But somewhere in the depth of my feelings there is a conflict: "You can't just stand there without being able to defend yourself. You should defend the freedom of your nation to the very last." Above all, however, I love our country too much to have it made into a battleground for the superpowers. I am not as afraid of the danger of communism as I am of the danger of weapons. I feel that the peace movement is extremely important. And I think it is equally important that we women should be listened to. Women never wanted war. They have always been the victims.

MARTA KARPF

Born in 1919, the eldest of four. Has severe back problems and difficulty walking, a result of doing heavy farmwork during the war. Married 1946. Has two sons. Husband suffered from war injuries and died in 1975.

1985

Wartime

The Farm

I grew up on a beautiful farm, the eldest of four children. When I was sixteen years old I had to work like a man — and I was proud that I was able to do it. During the very first year of the war both my brother and my fiancé were killed in action. Nobody asked how we could manage the farm without them. We grew corn, wheat, rye, beets, potatoes and tobacco that had to be tilled and harvested. There were also meadows, vineyards, the house and the animals to be attended to.

In order to direct the bombers away from the city of Stuttgart, the army put up an imitation of the Stuttgart railway station in the middle of our land. They installed lights so that the bomber pilots would unload their deadly freight over our fields instead of over the city of Stuttgart. Because of this we couldn't use any machines to work in the fields. Everything had to be done by hand. It wasn't possible to leave the land fallow because we were required to meet delivery quotas of everything we grew. Every square inch of land was needed. Sometimes we worked out there till late in the night.

Towards the end of the war my parents became weaker and weaker, until they couldn't cope with the hard farmwork any longer. When my father broke both his legs and my mother acquired a heart condition I had to do most of the work alone, although both of them tried to help me as best they could.

In the fall of 1944 low-flying fighter planes attacked us while we were working in the fields. Since we no longer had a horse (all horses were confiscated by the military) we brought in the crops with a team of oxen. Each time the planes started shooting, the oxen became very nervous. Again and again they turned the wagon upside down, leaving its wheels in the air.

My father, in spite of his not being able to walk, went out to the fields with me to calm the animals while I worked. When he was there I didn't feel lonely. Once we went out with the oxen to bring in straw. Father was up on the wagon while I loaded the straw. We had almost finished when we heard and soon could see the bombers coming closer. We watched the bombs as they fell. They came down over our heads and exploded in a field not far from us. The oxen, whose names were Max and Fritz, raised their tails and started running, completely out of their senses. I grabbed Max's rein but neither he nor Fritz paid any attention to me. They kept running and dragged me with them all the way back to the stable. My arms and legs were bleeding. My mother looked at me with tears in her eyes when she saw me like that, but she couldn't say anything.

It was especially dangerous when the fighter planes attacked when we were in the vineyards. The planes came zooming down over the hills, and the gunners shot at us with their machine guns. The sheep that were grazing nearby ran up into the vineyard and tried to hide under our skirts. We squatted beside the low stone walls of our vineyard many times and thought we would never return home.

During the last weeks of the war, German soldiers installed their combat command center in our barn. During the night of April 6-7, 1945, the enemy shot artillery shells into our village for hours. In the morning, our house was hit and started burning. Father and I tried to extinguish the fire with water from several big tubs in the yard. While we were fighting the fire, the shells kept whistling over our heads. Now, every night we girls and a few old men who had not been drafted fought the fires. Other people gathered in air raid shelters. Eventually we ran out of water. We made a human chain to the river to bring water up to the village. The shooting went on and on. We didn't get any sleep during these days. When we looked up for a moment we saw that other villages were burning too.

The following night an SS officer came into our cellar, which served as an air raid shelter where several people had taken refuge. Only one loaf of bread was left on the shelf, and the officer wanted to take it. I told him that this was our last bread and that because of the shooting we were not able to do any baking now. I asked him to please leave the bread to the people in the shelter who were hungry too. I told him that we were sick and tired of this war, and asked why the soldiers didn't go home. While I spoke he slowly took out his gun and pointed it at my chest. My father reacted quickly. With his walking stick he hit the officer's hand hard. The gun fell to the ground. Suddenly, the officer was surrounded by German soldiers. I don't know where they came from. The officer gave my father a surprised look but didn't say anything. My father, leaning heavily on his two sticks, said, "Leave my daughter in peace. She has suffered enough. She lost her brother and her fiancé, and she has been working harder than two strong men." The officer turned around and left without another word.

That night I understood that I would have to bake bread. Too many hungry eyes kept staring at the last loaf on the shelf, which I cut up and distributed to the people in the shelter. Hurriedly I filled a big bowl with flour, added some water and yeast, and started to knead the dough. I worked by the light of one candle. It was supposed to be totally dark. I fetched wood and sneaked over to the oven. Taking care not to be seen, I lit a fire and then went back and divided the dough into seven beautiful loaves. When I went to pick up the baking tins which hung on the wall near the stable, my father saw me. He helped me carry the loaves and put them in the oven. This was the first time in his life that he had worked in the kitchen. After an hour the bread was baked. When we came back with the fresh bread which smelled so good, everybody was glad that I had made it.

On April 12, two artillery shells destroyed our house. One of them went all the way down to the basement. Surrounded by a cloud of dust and debris, we ran outside pulling Father and Mother with us. We sought shelter in the neighbor's house. At dawn we went back and saw that it was impossible to stay in our house any longer. The roof had — once again — come down, and inside everything was turned to rubble. We had experienced enough. With tears in our eyes, we put up a white sheet of surrender. Enemy troops marched through our village with guns pointed at the people. Tanks plowed through our fields.

That day, with a simple ceremony, we buried the people of our village who had been killed during the fighting, along with the dead German soldiers whom the military had left behind.

Born in 1931, in Hamburg. During her early childhood spent many nights in air raid shelters. Worked for fifteen years as a secretary in a publishing company in Heilbronn. Became a pacifist and peace activist. Married. Has three daughters.

The Americans Enter Our Town

*I*n Grandmother's little house in Frankenbach, now a suburb of Heilbronn, I lived through the entry march of the victors and the collapse of the Hitler empire.

It was night. A weird rumbling and a great tension were in the air. The rumbling came from the approaching tanks, and the tension from the fear. Who would come? We had heard terrible rumors about the arrival of troops. Which soldiers would come to our town — Americans, French, or the French Moroccan soldiers who had a reputation of being especially cruel? (I had never seen dark-skinned people and had a crazy fear of them.)

The clattering grew louder and the windowpanes rattled. Gigantic tanks came up the street making a racket and then stopped, because here the road ended, right in front of our little house. My grandmother sat trembling in a corner of the kitchen, and I hid myself behind a door. I wanted my mother, but she lay in a hospital after a bad accident. I held my breath, then the door was shoved in and tall soldiers pointing machine guns pushed their way through the narrow hall into our kitchen. What now?

Then a remarkable thing happened: The "Amis" [the Americans] didn't look at us, but directed all their attention toward our black stove and the hanging pots. One soldier laid his gun on the kitchen table and bent over the stove. He tried to light a fire. It was soon apparent that although American soldiers know how to handle machine guns, pistols and other weapons, they had no talent for handling a tricky Swabian coal stove. Soon smoke billowed from all its joints and cracks, and the soldiers coughed and cursed. Suddenly an American lifted his gun high and pointed it at my grandmother. She stood up trembling and pale as death, and raised her hands. The soldier pushed her to the stove. Relieved, we realized that this guy — tall as a tree — didn't want to shoot the tiny woman; instead he needed her help. Grandmother went into action and made kindling with a kitchen knife, and soon the stove began to hiss and crackle. A soldier got out the big pan and fried corned beef in it. A wonderful fragrance of cooked meat filled the kitchen, and the tension dissolved.

So our enemies were also people like us, who were hungry. They offered us some of the food, but we refused steadfastly. I, a German girl brought up from childhood in the spirit of Hitler to be faithful to the Fatherland, would not accept the tiniest bite from our enemies! Though my stomach growled, I felt myself to be a heroine. My grandmother also refused the attractive offer, but for other reasons. She admitted to me later that she was afraid of being poisoned. It wasn't until years later that I realized the comedy of this situation.

After this stop in our kitchen, the tank soldiers pulled out again, and we were very relieved. Unfortunately the troops that came after them did not behave so politely. They searched all the houses, and afterwards the residents found that many valuable possessions were missing. But this did not seem so important to us. Most important was that the war had ended. We could breathe again.

Born in 1933, in Heilbronn. Worked in a large factory that manufactured knitwear. Married in 1956. Has three children. Her husband, Manfred, lost his mother and sister in the bombing of Heilbronn. His father was also killed in the war.

Black Soldiers

After the December 4, 1944 bombing, we moved to Wimmental, a small village outside Heilbronn. A farm family made a room available for us, in which we lived until the end of the war.

The German army was already moving east in retreat when soldiers of the Waffen-SS came to us in the house. They ordered my father to transport something with the truck — what it was I don't know. My father refused. Then one soldier said to him: "We'll come back, after the war is over and we have won, and then you'll be the first one to be shot." My mother and we children feared for my father's life. The Waffen-SS might retake two or three towns, we thought, and then they would certainly carry out this threat.

A few days after this incident we were sitting in the kitchen in the evening when all at once there was a knock at the door. Several Americans came into the room with pointed weapons. "Here German soldiers?" they asked. When we said no, they stuck a gun in my father's back and made him walk in front of them while they searched the house. Our entire family was locked in the potato cellar for several days because the Americans requisitioned the house. It wasn't bad for us children during these days. All year long we had seen no chocolate, and now our enemies gave us some.

After a few days the soldiers went on. We children stood at the edge of the road and watched as the tanks of the advancing troops rolled through Wimmental. For the first time in my life I saw black people. The older children, whose word we believed, had told us they were cannibals. But nothing happened. The unit went by us quite peacefully.

Born in 1927, in Heilbronn. Immigrated to the United States in 1956. Currently employed as accountant clerk by Manitowoc County in Wisconsin. Widowed. Has two sons.

1950

The Homecoming

*A*fter being drafted into the German Labor Force [*Reichsarbeitsdienst*] in the fall of 1944, I was trained as a searchlight operator in southern Germany and then stationed in the greater Nürnberg area. We all knew that the end of the war was near. Finally, on April 16, 1945, the American army took over the little village in which we were stationed, after a short but fierce battle.

Four days later, on my eighteenth birthday, my two friends Anne and Herta and I decided that we should head for home. The three of us could travel together for about half of our trek; then I would have to continue on my own, as we were from different areas of Germany. Since the railroad system was all but destroyed and we had no other means of transportation, we would have to travel on foot and carry our few belongings. There was no mail delivery and we were anxious to see our families and have them know that we were alive.

We packed our belongings, such as they were. Our landlady provided us with some bread and canned sausage left over from our small camp, and we started for home early on April 21.

After a few hours' walk we met two young German soldiers who had been released from the army and were on their way home. Both were from the Rhineland region and we all could travel together for some distance. Most of the roads were in very poor condition. Numerous air raids and ground battles had left their marks everywhere and made foot-travel difficult. Many of the main roads were impassable and we had to detour, which added extra time and miles to our trip. Everywhere were American army vehicles and soldiers. Some of them waved to us and even offered us rides, which we always declined; others were hostile. The weather was typical for April — sometimes pleasant sunshine, sometimes rain or snow.

After the Occupation began, the American forces decreed a curfew for all German civilians, which meant that we had to be off the roads before sunset and find shelter for the night. Since we traveled mostly through small villages and rural areas, it was not too difficult to find a place to stay. Once we had an offer to spend the night in a barn, sleeping in the hayloft; other nights we girls spent in the security and comfort of a home, maybe on a sofa, or — what luxury — in a soft, warm featherbed. In the morning our hosts usually shared their milk, malt coffee and bread with us, sometimes even an egg. We had forgotten what they tasted like! Nobody had a lot, but everybody was willing to share with those who had even less. Very few rural homes had bathrooms in those days, so we washed ourselves with some cold water in a washbowl or, once or twice, in a wooden trough, taking turns pumping water for each other.

On the third day we had come to the point where we had to part ways. My three traveling companions would continue their trek in a northwesterly direction while I had to go by myself due west. We all stood around exchanging addresses and shaking hands, when a man approached us and asked about our plans. When he heard that I was on my way to Heilbronn, my hometown, he told me about a family who lived nearby with him and his wife after being evacuated from their home in Heilbronn. He told me to go to his house and visit with this family. After a final goodbye I left my friends and went to see the family I had been told about. During our visit they told me about another native of Heilbronn who had been evacuated to a neighboring village together with her eight-year-old son. I went to see this lady, who was anxious to go back home but was afraid to travel alone with just a young child. She was very happy to have found a traveling companion. She would be ready to leave in three days. I promised to wait. Mrs. W., the wife of the man I had met on the street, was kind enough to let me stay at their house for three days in exchange for some housework. I was exhausted and needed the rest; my sore feet bothered me, and it felt good not to have to wear hard shoes for a few days and give the blisters a chance to heal.

After three days, Mrs. B., my new traveling companion, came to pick me up and we went on our way. Mrs. B. had packed an old baby buggy with canned goods, and her little son pulled a small four-wheeled cart with other belongings in which I found room for my suitcase. We took turns pushing the buggy and pulling the wagon, often with little Wolfgang sitting on top. It did not take long before my feet were blistered again and every step was torture, but with every step we took we came a little closer to home. At one point we had to cross a creek, but the bridge had been destroyed. The natives of the nearby village had somehow managed to place several large rocks in the small river. In order to cross it, we had to hop from one rock to another. We made several trips to deposit our belongings on the other side, and finally to carry and pull our vehicles across. After reloading our carts, we continued on our way.

On April 30, we had come close to Heilbronn and it felt good to see familiar sights and to know that we had only a few more kilometers to go. But ahead of us there was a long, winding, uphill road and suddenly I felt like I was going to collapse. I sat down and tearfully told my traveling companion that I could not go on. She pulled me under a tree where we rested for awhile. When I felt better, we went on. Finally, we reached our destination — we were in Heilbronn. But the sight of our beloved hometown was shocking: most of the city was destroyed, either by bombs, fires, or artillery fire, and had it not been for a hill with a tower on top which had survived the turmoil, we would not have recognized our once beautiful, proud city.

There were very few natives to be seen, but everywhere there were foreign solders and former prisoners of war who celebrated their newfound freedom by getting drunk. We were shocked and frightened. My own family had been evacuated earlier in the year and I was not sure if they had returned to Heilbronn or were still living with some relatives in the country. Since I was afraid to go to my house alone, I decided to leave the city the next morning, hoping I would find my family in the country. First, though, we decided to go to my companion's mother's house, where I would stay for the night. On the way there we had a frightening experience.

When we were almost at our destination, we encountered a man carrying a jug of wine, obviously drunk. He asked us what time it was. When my friend looked at her watch, the man grabbed her by the wrist and threatened her with a knife he had pulled from his pants pocket. Mrs. B. tore herself away from him and screamed for help. The man got scared, took his jug and ran off. This was not the way we had pictured our homecoming. Quite shaken, we arrived at her mother's house. There I spent the night in a room which had a man-size hole in the outside wall, made by artillery fire and covered with cardboard. I was scared to sleep there, but the night went without incident.

The next morning, I and Mrs. B., who had decided to accompany me partway and visit relatives, left for the village where I hoped to find my family. Along the way we passed a field where a farmer and his family were having lunch. They invited us to join them and we gratefully accepted. While we were sitting at the edge of the field, several open trucks went slowly past, filled with German soldiers, now prisoners of war in their own country. They waved to us and we waved back and held our partly eaten pieces of bread up to them. They accepted it eagerly. We all were hungry, but they needed the food more than we!

After Mrs. B. arrived at her destination, we parted and I went the rest of the way by myself. Early in the afternoon I arrived at the village where I hoped to find my family alive and well. Full of anxiety I walked toward my relatives' house. I wondered if I would find them there, if they had survived the chaos, or if they had fallen victim to this horrible war like my oldest brother who, at age nineteen, lost his life in Russia. Or my best friend, or my neighbor, or other people I had known who lost their lives on the homefront.

Then I saw Marlies, my six-year-old sister, who apparently recognized me and ran into the house to tell my mother I was coming. We had a joyful reunion and I was very happy to see everybody alive. We did not know the fate of a brother who had been in the German army, but, as we learned later, he had been kept prisoner in some camp and was released unharmed months later.

My long trip had finally come to an end, and the end of the war was declared just a few days later. We had lost the war, but it was over at last. May there never be another war!

Born in 1925, in the Soviet Union. Deported to Germany in 1942. Widowed in 1977. Has three children. Recently returned to the Soviet Union for the first time since deportation.

Farewell Forever

I was born in December 1925, in Taganrog on the Sea of Azof, in the southwestern part of the Soviet Union. When World War II began I was a young girl of fifteen and was attending a technical school where I was learning airplane construction. During the summer of 1941 I was preparing for second-semester examinations. One evening around nine, when my family was at home — my father was reading the newspaper, my stepmother was doing needlework, the rest of the family was already in bed — we heard planes overhead but did not think twice about it. Then suddenly there were three explosions, one after the other. My father called for us children, then there was an appalling bang, the lights went out and we screamed. We children lay on the floor and my father covered us with his body. Suddenly everything was silent, with the exception of the sound of an airplane flying away. There was the smell of dust and gas in the air.

We did not sleep that night — we were too frightened. The bombs had exploded fifty meters away from our house. The house of my girlfriend was hit and her mother was killed. Fortunately my girlfriend had been staying with her aunt at the time. In the morning we heard over the radio and through the loudspeakers on the streets that Hitler had attacked our border despite the treaty that he had signed with Stalin.

From then on we received training at school in loading and aiming guns, using grenades and using gas masks. When second semester began in September we could not study well, for fear of what would happen to our homeland. The German army was approaching. We students were mobilized to dig trenches and were relocated fifty-five kilometers to the west. We could clearly hear the explosion of artillery as the German army approached. Airplanes bombed our area more frequently. Suddenly, one night our leaders left secretly and we did not know where they had gone. Afraid and wanting to go home to be with our parents, my friends and I ran all night long. When I got home my mother said that my father was away helping to evacuate people from the collective farms. My four-teen-year-old brother had voluntarily signed up to go to the front. Upon hearing this news I cried.

I remained in Taganrog with my stepmother, my grandmother and my two younger stepsisters. On October 17, 1941, our city was occupied by the German army. There were terrible street battles. We spent two days and one night in our cellar. The city was severely damaged and there were no jobs as winter approached. There was great hunger in the town, since little harvesting had been done and the Red Army destroyed everything edible as they withdrew so the German soldiers would have nothing to eat. The cattle had been driven to the east. We gathered half-burned wheat, ground it with a coffee machine, and made porridge and bread out of it. We were able to keep one room warm in the house by burning coal which had been dropped from the train. Winter came and it was exceedingly cold but there was almost no snow. Nights were as light as the days, which gave the Red Army an advantage in bombing German bases. In our city there were many partisans. One day in January as I was walking to school for my German class, I saw the bodies of many Russian civilians who had been hung in a big open square in front of the railroad station. Later we found out that a German SS officer had been shot by a Partisan. The Germans had a slogan, "One German —

ten Russians," and they kept their word.

At the end of January 1942, an SS leader and his aide were assigned to live in our house. They were decent soldiers. Grandmother cooked and washed for them and we received money for their board in return. Grandmother said: "They are also human and have mothers that cry about them in Germany." Adjunct Hans T. was from Königsberg and he got along with Grandmother especially well. He often told her that Hitler was crazy — not normal. And slowly I began to understand that most Germans did not want war either, but that they were forced into it.

In our school there were many Jewish boys and girls. By the spring of 1942 most of the Jews were gone and we did not know why. Through our best student, Kurt, we learned of the persecution of the Jews. Kurt had to hide at his grandmother's because his mother was Jewish. It was said that the Jews were being taken outside of the town and shot. We did not know why. It was horrible.

In February 1942, my sister Angelika was born, and that she was able to grow up in those times was a miracle. We did not have any milk, only porridge made from burnt wheat, and a few grains of corn and sunflower seeds which we traded for goods in the village.

In the beginning of April, Adjutant Hans T. helped my mother get a job in a German bakery in our town. It was a hard job, but we had bread and our lives were getting back to normal when a card arrived in the mail which was to change my whole life. It was just a small card. Single people between the ages of sixteen and thirty-five had to register with the German commander. Whoever refused would be severely punished — that meant shot. My mother was horrified, but there was nothing to be done. She asked our SS officer to intercede, but he couldn't help. We had to appear for a superficial medical examination and all of us who were relatively healthy received marching orders.

On April 25, 1942, we young people stood in front of the destroyed railway station and waited for our names to be read from a list. I was ordered to go to Germany for half a year. Girls were to take with them one dress, one pair of shoes, underwear, and food for a couple of days. We were to leave the following day at six-thirty in the morning. I was accompanied to the appointed meeting place by my grandmother, stepmother, and two little sisters — Tamara, age six, and Linda, age three. Awaiting us at the meeting place were the German military police, who were referred to as "Kettenhund" [chain-dog] because of the chain collars they wore. Our families were allowed to walk with us to the end of the town; then, at the bridge, we had to say good-bye. When Grandmother and Mother cried, six-year-old Tamara tried to comfort them by saying, "Elli is coming back this evening." Yes, that was my farewell forever. I never saw my grandmother and my mother again. Grandmother died in 1962 and Mother died in 1976.

Guarded by the military police, we walked one hundred fifty kilometers, because the railroad track had been destroyed between Taganrog and Stalino. If people tried to hide or escape, they were shot. We heard the shots. Apart from the bread that we had brought from home, there was nothing to eat. We could wash only when we came to a stream or a little river. Not having been allowed to rest for any length of time, we were exhausted when we reached the city of Stalino, where we were loaded into a railroad cattle-car and transported further west. The car was opened only every couple of days. At that time pails were emptied and we were allowed to wash in a little river. Every two or three days we were given a little bit of bread and some hot barley soup which was very diluted. In Litzmannstadt we were stripped and deloused; in order to get our clothes back we had to parade naked in front of two groups of German soldiers. It was very humiliating. We were only sixteen years old.

We crossed the Polish border and after three weeks, on May 16, 1942, arrived in Trier where we were locked inside a school. That afternoon some German women came to select workers. They turned us to the right and to the left and looked at us from head to foot as though we were slaves. I was assigned to a large farm where we had to work very hard and bear many humiliations. Just as the Jews had to wear their star, we had to wear a blue patch with the word "East" in white letters. We were not allowed to write home. I was lucky because before I had left home Adjunct Hans T., who was still living in my parents' house, had given me his field postal number and said that I should write to him and he would give the letters to my mother. We handled it that way until he died in battle in 1943.

I came to know a Dutch family who owned a radio and worked on a nearby farm. We would meet secretly at night, listen to the radio, and rejoice when we heard that the German army was losing and was being forced to withdraw. One morning a man from the Gestapo came and forced several of us to go with him on the train to Trier. At first we didn't know why. Later on we found out that someone had heard us listening to the radio and reported us. We were interrogated day and night. Some of us were beaten — we heard the screams in the cellar. A few days after that my girlfriend and I were taken out of the cellar and forced to do work like polishing the shoes of the Gestapo soldiers. In the hall there was a list of names of those who were to be set free, those who were going to be sent to a concentration camp, and those who were to remain there. We would read the list, then prepare the others who could not see it for what was to happen. We were all afraid of the concentration camp. After we had spent about two weeks in prison, my girlfriend and I were picked up and taken back to the large farm. I was glad to be back on the farm.

Other Russians were forced to work in armament factories where they produced bombs which would be used for the destruction of their own people. In the fall of 1943 I was ordered to work as a translator in one of these factories. Food there was heavily rationed and my weight dropped to one hundred pounds. Sometimes we could not even stand up straight because we were so tired and hungry. On Sundays we went to a farmer and begged. We ate the bread which was given to us, even though it was moldy. I wrote to the farm where I had been living and begged Frau M. to come and pick me up. She came and took me back to the farm, where I remained until September 1944, when I was ordered to live with a family in the town of Kinlein on the Mosel River. I looked after the three children and was treated kindly. At last I was relieved of the dull physical work and found some challenge for my mind.

The German army suffered more and more losses, and by March 1945 the Americans and the Russians had advanced nearly to Kinlein. One day we workers from the East were ordered to the marketplace. The family for whom I worked advised me and my girlfriend not to go, and they hid us under some hay in a barn. Later we found out that those workers from the East who had gone to the marketplace had been taken to the woods and shot.

In April, when the Americans arrived, we were assembled in a camp. There were Italians, French, Dutch, Russians, Poles, etc., all hoping to be sent home. Later I was transferred to a special camp that had been created just for us Russians. Conditions there were miserable — for days at a time we did not get anything to eat or drink. The commanding officer was an American captain. I was one of a few girls he took from the camp to work in his kitchen. We were better off there; at least we had food to eat.

Once a week a group of workers from the East were deported from Germany by the Russian occupying forces. I was completely perplexed to learn that the people who were being sent back to Russia were not allowed to return to their homes. Instead they were sent to the mines as punishment for having worked for the Germans. I have thought a great deal about this over the years and I have never been able to understand why we were punished twice, initially by the Germans and again by the Russians. Hadn't we already suffered enough?

Fortunately, the American commanding officer for whom my girlfriend and I worked, took us away from the camp. To conceal my identity I was given a Polish name, Mandrowski. Poles were not persecuted as much as we Russians were by our own people. We were advised not to write to our families for fear that they would be punished. Thus it was that I traveled with the Allies until the company was disbanded in November 1946. I washed dishes and clothes, delivered the mail, worked in the PX, and set tables in the canteen. My girlfriend married an American in 1943. That was out of the question for me because I wanted to go back home.

After the American company left I found work in a lumber yard in Mannheim and continued to live under my assumed name. In the summer of 1947 I met Hans, my husband-to-be. His parents could not tolerate his relationship with a foreigner, so we met secretly. In 1950 I found out that I was pregnant. After long discussions, his family allowed us to get married, in September, one week before the birth of our first child, a daughter. We did not get married in a church because my husband was ashamed of having a foreign wife. I had to constantly put up with accusations from my husband as well as from his mother. When my husband became an alcoholic, there was little money and I was responsible for looking after the family. In 1952 we had a son. At this time my mother-in-law suddenly insisted it was important for the children to be baptized, so my husband and I had to be married in the church.

In 1953, after General Stalin's death, amnesty was issued to the Russian workers, thereby making a return to the Soviet Union possible. I let a couple of years pass before finally writing home in 1956. My family was incredibly happy when they received my letter. Up until then they thought that I had died or been murdered by the Germans. When another daughter was born to my parents in 1947, they gave her my first name in remembrance of me.

In 1954 my third child, a daughter, was born. My father-in-law loved the children very much. My husband drank more and more and I had to work hard in order to support the family. My father wrote telling me that I ought to come home and that we would survive somehow. However, I knew that his wife, my stepmother, did not want me to live there. I did not know what to do. Life in Germany was hell. My husband beat me and the children frequently.

In 1960 I decided to return to the Soviet Union, for good! I packed seven suitcases and went with the children to the Russian consulate in Bonn. After getting the appropriate papers, we drove to Berlin. There, in the consulate, I was asked whether I really wanted to go back. Yes, I wanted to go home to the Soviet Union, but I began to have second thoughts. Here the children were at home; there the family and the environment would be strange. I had to think of my children. Thus I went back to Neuenstadt, and left the future up to fate. I divorced my husband in 1970 after the children had grown up.

I wanted to depict in my story the damage that war can cause, the uprooting of a human being. I am a foreigner in both Germany and the Soviet Union. I don't belong anywhere. I speak German with a Russian accent and Russian with a German accent. I am neither German or Russian. What am I?

Born 1949. Teaches German and history at senior high school level. Married. Has one daughter.

1988

In the Stocks

For weeks after reading the account of your ordeal in Jacobi's book [see excerpt that follows], dear sister, you took possession of me. I could only see things from your perspective, from the perspective of the stocks. But I could not comprehend why the townspeople of forty years ago — so full of destructive lust — spat in your face and threw stones, and why the hate of thousands who gathered in the marketplace was directed against you and not against the brutal Nazi stalwarts of Heilbronn. I could also not understand why your tormentors employed the rituals of a witch-craft trial in the middle of the twentieth century. Did they believe you had celebrated a Witch's Sabbath with the Pole — or were they

129

afraid you could destroy their mad order of life? You so bravely defied the inhuman laws of the Nazis by showing affection for a ragged, undernourished "sub-human."

I wanted to search for you to find out if you are still alive or if they let you die so as not to have to bother with you anymore. From you, your friends or your family, I could learn about what cruel behavior people are capable of when oppressed by a political system. We could learn from your story, because at that time Europe had gone out of control. Today the world is in the process of learning about it.

To track you down, I asked dedicated historians of local Heilbronn history who have published works on the Nazi period about your case. I wanted to know who betrayed you, but most of all I wanted to know your name, so that I could ask at the city registry if you are still alive. The local historians couldn't answer my questions. They had heard anecdotes about you, but during the war years when Party members went on witch-hunts in Heilbronn, they were all in concentration camps, prisons or at the front. One professor, however, was able to support my research by giving me advice, searching for eyewitnesses and directing me to the archives where the local newspaper, the Heilbronner *Tagblatt*, was kept almost in its entirety. But during the war years there were almost no reports in the local section about particularly brutal activities by the Brown Shirts, such as the torture of political dissenters in the basements of the Gestapo or excesses against Jews. The local editors presented their readers with stories about honest and upright public officials with whom they could identify. So nothing is written of your humiliation nor about the rampaging Nazis who needed props from the torture chamber to maintain their power.

From time to time there are reports of draconian sentences against women who broke the Nazi law forbidding contact with war prisoners. The prison terms were often very long, apparently applied legally by judges who have never had to account for their acts. But since your punishment was most probably not initiated by a court but by the Party, former functionaries must have known your name and the background of the spectacle. They must have carefully prepared the show during their meetings. I therefore wrote politely for information to all the Nazi leaders I knew about, but I received not a single response. They were shielded from me in their lovely homes and splendid gardens by their wives or secretaries or daughters. They likely had good reason to be silent.

I became impatient, I wasn't making progress. I encouraged friends and acquaintances to find some trace of you; I was after them constantly. I spoke to at least a hundred pleasant-looking older people on the bus, in stores and in the townhall square. Most of them were very reserved, many quickly turned away from me, some insulted me. Quite a few knew of you, but nothing specific. Surprisingly, though, they all said you took your own life. In some versions you drank pesticide or hydrochloric acid; in others you hanged yourself on a big fir tree or turned on the gas valve. As best I can piece the story together, your Polish boyfriend was shot by uniformed men on the Kopfer [a brook not far from the city]. Here are some extracts about you from conversations taken down for me by friends in the Workshop of Women for Peace:

"I lived on Schillerstrasse and was just a child. We went to the marketplace because we wanted to see the show. The entire square and the Kaiserstrasse were full. The woman was led through the entire city on foot, by two men. People spat at her and called her whore and other obscenities. I had the feeling that no one was against what went on and that the people were pleased." (Frau F.)

"The people were very excited. I was also there, but when I saw her face I knew that she was a common whore who carried on with everyone. No harm done. It isn't worth making a big thing out of it."(Frau G.)

"People came from surrounding villages to see the show. Maybe she was out of line; you don't do that when your husband and brother are in the field." (Frau R.)

"In 1941 I was an apprentice in a shop on Main Street and I witnessed the whole affair. The woman was led through the crowd on an oxcart. There was a man in front of the cart beating on a tub. The woman was about thirty-five or forty years old and had long black hair. Such events keep coming to mind during one's whole life." (Frau Z.)

I am astonished that most of the women watching were not morally outraged by the type of punishment you received. They didn't see the humiliation of their own sex in your degradation, nor that they had been reduced to nothing more than the "property" of the male of the Nordic master race, at his free disposal, to be punished when they dared to break his taboos. All attempts at women's emancipation ended in the stocks.

I first became aware of just how great the intimidation of women was, in April 1984, after an article appeared with an appeal from the Workshop of Women for Peace to all readers who knew about your case and others like yours to get in touch with me. It is odd, dear sister, that since that time I've lost sight of you as I learn of the horrible fates of other women at the time.

At least twenty people, for the most part women, contacted me in response to the appeal. From four callers I learned that many more women had their hair shorn, though with less ceremony and audience than you. My informers lived near the abused women during the war and knew their names. Two of the women were certain that their earlier acquaintances had died in the meantime. The two others had lost track of their old neighbors in the '60s. Pity for the victims and decades of suppressed anger against the tormentors moved these women to call me. They encouraged me to bring the crimes against your sisters into the light of day.

One woman told me of a forty-year-old woman in an outlying area who had her hair shorn because she slipped some food to a Russian. The woman was very poor herself and acted purely out of pity. Another caller recounted that a farmer's wife, forced to manage the farm during the war with a prisoner of war because her husband was at the front, was beaten by Party members until she admitted to having an affair with the foreign laborer. Her hair was cut off in her own house. The laborer disappeared without a trace.

A further case was told as follows: a young, single, very beautiful woman was considered standoffish by her peers, who envied her because of her long dark hair and her proud carriage. She was supposed to have been rather reserved toward men. An awkward, unattractive man — most likely longing for her body — testified at the Brown House [the local Nazi party headquarters] that he had caught her with a Frenchman. As a result, that evening on her way home she was attacked by a horde of uniformed men and seriously beaten.

And finally I heard about a young secretary who met a war prisoner working as a translator in her office and had a child by him. This woman had her hair shorn and was mistreated by the Nazis toward the end of her pregnancy.

I didn't receive any concrete information from the majority of the callers, who were probably members of the victims' families. They all wanted to remain anonymous and requested or demanded aggressively that I not publish anything about these incidents. This was a typical call:

"Why are you writing about it after almost forty years? You can't publish that. The whole countryside is talking about it. The woman has had serious heart trouble for the past five days (since the article appeared in the newspaper *Heilbronner Stimme*). She's afraid her grandchildren could find out."

What woman? Why shouldn't the grandchildren find out? Did I really cause her to become sick by writing about the crimes committed against her? Do I have the right to continue my research when I might cause such suffering? I leave out all the names in my account and cross out every concrete reference in order not to hurt you all again. But why are you so well-protected? Can it be that your families are ashamed because of you? That in forty years they've learned nothing? Listen to the response that one of our Workshop members got to her inquiry about your victimization:

> *Questioner:* "I'm calling for the Workshop of Women for Peace—"
>
> *Respondent (interrupting):* "Well, I've had enough of you. I read the article about you in the *Heilbronner Stimme*. You know, all the people who are for the foreigners today, who even want to give them the right to vote — they're ruining Germany. Back then I had a completely different idea of what Germany could become. But today they let in all the refugees and the Turks too. Things are so bad today that a German apprentice has to compete with a Turk for a place on the workbench. If that's how they want it, they should just open all the borders and they'll bring in the hashish and dominate our lives. But you shouldn't call that Germany anymore. Also, I'd really like to know where you got my name. Who gave it to you? That really bothers me. You know, I was against Hitler, I have it in writing. I was fourteen years old when he came to power. I didn't elect him, but I had to suffer because he was elected. I raised my son alone back then. No one helped me. I was alone. Today I never speak about those days, nothing comes out of me. I've been through enough. Consider me dead, you'll learn nothing from me. Good-bye!"

Although the Workshop caller had made no reference to foreign workers, this respondent answered automatically, with the right-wing slogans of your former tormentors. She and other women were tortured to such an extent that they took on the ideology of those who punished you. They don't have the strength to resist, because their powers of resistance were broken long ago. It has been observed in the dictatorships of Latin America, whose torture chambers were shaped by SS officers and people from the Gestapo, that after serious beatings the flayed victims identify with their torturers, after losing their own personalities.

The terrorizing of women who dared to have a relationship with a non-German continued after the war. In 1946 a teacher was held down by a gang of men who cut off her hair because she had been seen with an American soldier. A long trail of sawdust was scattered in front of the homes of girls who had contact with Black Americans. These examples are most probably only the tip of the iceberg, because the victims so often remain silent. For socio-psychological reasons it is impossible for them to publicly denounce the wrong done to them. But why are their families ashamed along with them? Are the families of the perpetrators ashamed as well? Why hasn't a district attorney prosecuted the criminals of his sex who humiliated you women so much that your later life was ruined? Why have the criminal acts of these men to this day not even damaged their social prestige? Have people's ways of thinking changed so little in the last decades?

[Uwe Jacobi, The Missing Records from Town hall, Heilbronn 1981, p. 88: From an entry in the diary of a teacher, September 1941.]

The marketplace fills within minutes. Laughter and jeering are in the air. Mayor Gultig lends a hand as the flowers are removed from the steps of the town hall.

Toward five o'clock the crowds become frightening. A man carrying a chair over his head makes his way through the throng. "She's sitting over there!" someone screams suddenly. The pushing and shoving become wild. Women shriek hysterically, children are almost smothered, a wolfhound chomps at the bit.

The show begins.

The thirty-nine-year-old woman, accused of having relations with a Pole, is lifted onto a truck and pushed into a chair. A few spit at the "penitent," biblical stones fly.

Suddenly a determined young man in overalls appears at her side. They say he works for the city. He hacks off her hair lock by lock with a giant pair of tailor's scissors. As each lock falls he presents the woman to the gaping population who roar each time.

The festival moves toward its climax. The "barber" switches to a two-millimeter shaver, then to a one-twentieth of a millimeter for the precision work. Her scalp turns into a billiard ball. She's shown to the people over and over. The defamed woman is expressionless, her face looks as if modeled out of clay.

Behind the author a young boy stands on his bike. "My whole life I've always hoped to see a woman without hair," the boy calls out. "It's just like I imagined it."

As the crowning glory to his act the man in overalls gives a speech to the people. "The time must come again," he announces with full conviction, "in which unprincipled women are stripped and whipped in the public marketplace in front of the entire council!"

That's not all the barber has to say. "German blood must be protected with all means acceptable to German sentiment."

It is later said the defamed woman, mother of two children, hung herself.

Epilogue:
A Letter to My Children

Y ou have asked me: "How is it that you were silent for so long? It's necessary that you, just you, say what you think."

As if that were so simple!

I want to tell you how it was. How everything came to pass as it did. I want to show you the long way that I had to go until today. Perhaps it can be of use to you. It was not a smooth way. It led me through peaks and valleys and also into many a dead end. I had to build bridges over nothing at an age in which my powers were not really adequate. Of course, everyone who stood on the edge of the abyss after the collapse but didn't want to be pulled in had to do this. Everyone experienced the external collapse together, and together they overcame it. Each one had to come to terms with the internal collapse alone.

What happened in me at that time — I could not then have put it into words. Also, everyone was too much concerned with himself or herself to pay attention to the difficulties of a child. No one then thought about the fact that children, too, not just adults, stood before the ruins of their world. Whoever thinks that children forget quickly is mistaken. The sublime words of the propaganda speakers buried themselves deep in my soul. Full of devotion I drew in the exciting words, was ready to dedicate and, if necessary, sacrifice my young life totally to the service of the Fatherland. I wore my blonde braid proudly and I was convinced of the greatness and the mission of the German people.

Did I understand what I believed? Is that important? For centuries people have believed the Church without understanding it. The promise of a better world is enough. Didn't all these gentlemen promise a better world? In any case, I wanted to fight to the last drop of blood to defend my German Fatherland against the cowardly superior power of the enemy.

When my mother hung a white sheet over the balcony as a sign of surrender, on April 20, 1945, the birthday of our Führer, it stabbed me like a knife. I felt shame and powerless rage. Oh, if I only had a weapon now! I would run out, I would shoot them all dead — those cowardly dogs! — until they shot me down. Yes, that's what I would do. To die in the face of the enemy, that would be noble, proud and bold, as is worthy of a German! How my mother prevented my actually doing this, I don't know anymore. In any case, I had become a fanatic National Socialist, a glowing devotee of our Führer. How could that happen? Quite normally, actually.

As the war began, I was barely six years old and my biggest problem was the problem of all elder sisters and brothers — sibling rivalry. My father had to join the army, and on August 27, 1939, when he left, my childhood went with him. He could do nothing about that, and neither could my mother. It was simply so.

I still remember how it was on the last day my father was at home. The sun was shining, it was warm and the dahlias were blooming in the garden. My sister was six months old, my brother four years old. We had a small house on the edge of the city and I think we were a happy family. My father photographed us all together. "So that you won't forget us," said my mother. "Why should you forget us?" I asked. He took me in his arms: "Because I have to leave. There is a war." "War?" I asked, "what is that?" Then suddenly the sirens howled. My father said, "Do you hear that? That is war." I thought a long time, but I didn't know what my father meant.

From now on my mother lived together with us children in the house that was suddenly much too big. Aside from us four, there were only a few chickens; somewhat later there were rabbits and a goat. Mother had a lot of work. She could hardly concern herself with me. Indeed, I was already "reasonable"; I was already at an age where I could help her. And I did what was expected of me. As small as I was, I still sensed that everything was too much for my mother, that she felt herself hardly mature enough to do all the tasks, make all the decisions alone. So I helped her as best I could, made no trouble for her, was "reasonable."

Evenings in bed I dreamed about my father. All happiness, everything bright, all play, my whole childhood had disappeared with him, very prematurely. In my dreams he had represented all that was great and strong; now that he was gone and unreachable, he took on superhuman proportions.

I became a very serious child. Much too young to be able to carry responsibility, I began to feel responsible nevertheless. Were the chickens fed, the windows darkened, should I dig potatoes, fetch ration cards . . .?

When you ask me today — "Why can't you play, Mother? Celebrate an occasion? Why can't you just let everything go once in a while?" — I think all this was irretrievably lost for me with the beginning of the Second World War.

I saw how my mother struggled. I had to help her, relieve her somehow. How could I have let things go then, play, celebrate? I unlearned the ability to play very quickly, and today I cannot learn it again. Having to play is like a nightmare for me. I can't do it. You had a hard time with me earlier, when you would have liked so much to play with me. Again and again you came with the games "Sorry" or "Old Maid" and I forced myself to play in order not to disappoint you — and I became ill or got a headache. I can't play. This is stronger than I am.

Meanwhile war became an everyday affair. To be sure, I didn't know what war actually was. The battles took place elsewhere, but war was something completely normal. One also got used to the absence of Father and the other men. Our life went on its orderly way, with ration cards, air-raid drills, blackouts. Once in a while one heard of fallen fathers or brothers. Then the women wore black and cried more than usual. But since these men weren't even there, this was hardly reality for us children.

In the summer of 1942 we could not imagine any other life. That our mother was continually overworked and never laughed and often cried was normal for us. Sometimes she fell asleep at the table when she sat and sewed on a rainy day. When her head fell to the placemat, making a loud noise, nothing and no one could wake her. We would say, "She's sleeping again. Why does she fall asleep all the time?" We dared not disturb her.

On the way home from school I frequently met the newspaper lady. She gave me a few newspapers to distribute on our little street, so that she could save herself going part of her route. I usually began reading while still in the street. There was something about "diminished gross tonnage," about "our brave boys and our glorious army," which had again encircled a city, leveled a town or torn apart an enemy division. I read about the heroes of our air force, who had caused the enemy high casualties, and I began to be proud of our victorious German soldiers.

There was hardly any other news, except for the obituaries. Most of these had the symbol of the Iron Cross, underneath which was printed the name and the words: "Died a hero's death for Führer, Folk and Fatherland," or something similar. I asked my mother: "What does that mean?" "That is the war," was her answer, as it was to most questions. "Is everything that's in the newspaper about the war?" I asked. "Yes, everything." "Then is the whole newspaper for the war? And if there is no war, then what? Is there no newspaper?" "When there is no war," she answered, "then there is peace, but you don't know at all what that is." And she left me standing.

She is probably crying again, I thought. One can't even talk with her. And I wished my father were there. I could have asked him, he would definitely have given me a real answer.

But my mother was right. I didn't even know what peace was.

At the beginning of the year 1944, I see myself for the first time in the uniform of a *Jungmädel* [young girls' organization], a believing young National Socialist, who was ready to go through fire for her Führer and her Fatherland. Together in the lodge-hall we heard, from now on, the patriotic speeches, sang Fatherland songs, or our leader read relevant texts to us. And the great words fell on fertile ground. We intoxicated ourselves with words like "national character," "custom," "readiness to sacrifice," "honor," "glory" and "victory" — always victory.

That more and more fathers and brothers were reported fallen or missing, that bombs fell, that food was more and more scarce, this was the sacrifice that we had to make for our people, because the cowardly enemy horde was without end. We believed with certainty that this was a necessary and just war for the freedom of our people. Death, suffering and misery we did not see. Indeed, we didn't even know that it could have been otherwise.

Meanwhile, I also thought I knew what war was — something

holy, something through which all the noble qualities of humanity that we were always being told about was fully realized. In war a man should prove himself! And to die a hero's death for the Fatherland seemed to me the highest that a man could wish. What a pity that I was not a man!

If Hitler had won the war, I don't know what would have become of us brainwashed children. But when the facade of the thousand-year empire began to crumble, and words like "greatness" and "final victory" lost their credibility, what was left was hate.

I hope you don't know what hate can call up in the soul of a child. I hope you will never learn it. Children are indeed complete people. What they are, what they feel, what they do, they do totally. When a child hates, then there is no place left for anything else. And hate does not die all that easily. How much energy it cost me to control this hatred, which produced its effects for years somewhere deep inside me and again and again showed up in a totally irrational way.

Meanwhile the war reached us, too. Bombs fell, low-flying fighter planes showed up in the sky, dead people lay in the streets. That didn't shock us children anymore. We had grown into it. We had no fear. We didn't realize at all what was happening. We even found the low-flyers very interesting. We had learned at school how we had to behave: at the first sound of the motor, when the airplane began to dive, we were to get down into the ditch, face down, holding our schoolbags over our heads with both hands, and stay down until the planes turned away again. We were not to move or look up. We considered all this an exciting game, bragged to each other later about how low "the flyer went right by me," how close the bullets struck. And we were lucky. We never learned that it was a deadly game.

April 1945, a few days before the war ended for us, for the first time I got a sense of what war really is. I saw three young German soldiers not so much older than myself, running for their lives. Were these the same boys that I had so ardently envied? There was no more courage, no more heroism, there was only fear left. An American tank broke out of the forest above and drove those young soldiers before it. With the fear of death in their faces, they ran, fled down into the street. They threw their weapons away and ran close by me. But they didn't see me. As I lost sight of them, they were still running. Like a ghost, the tank had disappeared again into the forest. Suddenly I noticed that I was crying. I had become very reflective. But events piled up and soon I had forgotten the three soldiers.

A few days later a white sheet hung from our balcony. We had capitulated. And I was still alive!

What followed now were years of hatred, years of rage. I simply could not accept that my Führer and his circle of advisors were criminals, that everything we had been told was false and lies, and that these healthy gum-chewing men who were the victors were downright friendly. They should be evil, should beat and kick us, then one could at least hate them properly, then my world view would have fit my reality.

That we were hungry, that I had no shoes — that was no tragedy for me. It was the same for everyone. But that these enemies that I hated so intensely were people like us, that one of them even gave me a pair of shoes — this I couldn't bear. And my mother even thanked him for them!

Hadn't she also hoisted the bedsheet of surrender, instead of dying a hero's death? Hadn't she gone, without resisting, taking pail and rag, when it was demanded that we clean the American officers' club? She had heated the wash-kettle in order to wash the underwear of American soldiers — instead of throwing their dirty socks at their feet!

From now on my mother was also drawn into the orgies of my hatred. On the outside I did everything that was necessary, as before. With gnashing teeth I helped to wash the mountains of laundry, clean the officers' club, but inside a volcano simmered. I felt myself powerless, humiliated, dirtied.

One day a man stood at our door, covered with dirt, starved, sick. He said: "Good day, are you all healthy?" and dragged himself straightaway to a chair. It was my father.

For almost six years I had dreamed of the shining, god-like young hero that he had become in my imagination. Now he too was no longer worth dreaming about. Now I had no one to admire. Was there no one who was still strong and proud and courageous? Everyone was weak and cowardly and afraid, and I began to despise them all. All.

I closed myself in, in my pride. The destruction of all my values now left behind a chaos of hatred and desire for revenge. I had nothing more, nothing onto which I could hold. Only shards left. My dreams were shattered, my faith was lies. Heroism and greatness, which I had been taught to love, were nowhere to be found. The people around me, my parents and all the others, seemed so wretched to me. They wanted nothing more than to live. For this they took upon themselves every humiliation. How could I still love them?

There was no way I could show them how I saw things. So that no one would come too close to me, I hit out in all directions. I, too, only wanted to live, apparently. Otherwise, in view of my inner rebellion, would I have helped my parents again and again, taken on myself everything that they took on in order to pull us through?

De-nazification. New nourishment for scorn, hatred and vengefulness. My father, too, made this "Journey to Canossa," as he called it. He had to do it. In any case, I couldn't and wouldn't understand that he had no other choice. I still believed the right thing would be to die for "Führer, Folk and Fatherland," waving the flag with one hand while raising the other in the Hitler salute. That alone seemed worthy of a German man to me — even if there was no longer any such thing as this Fatherland.

Yes, I was a fanatical little monster then. And I was unhappy and lonesome in my stubbornness. Today I know that I was not the only one. For many children it may have gone similarly. But this wasn't talked about. Each child had to work things out for itself.

Our parents were exhausted and helpless, and the school, which should have taken over the task of re-education, dragged from one provisional solution to another. The few teachers who were left were no better off than our parents. Their main concern was to glue together the pages in our books that had National Socialist texts. There was no civics instruction, and pains were taken so that in history class we stayed as long as possible in ancient times so that the school year could end punctually before the French Revolution.

I was eleven years old as the war ended. Four years later the new German Constitution went into effect, and the Federal Republic was established. That could have been a new beginning for us children who had been seduced by National Socialism, but it wasn't. We had been so strongly influenced and our mistrust had grown so great. The adults probably had no idea what destruction the Nazi period had caused in the children. In any case, I was still licking my wounds. I wanted nothing more to do with politics. Politics had ruined my childhood. How was I to know I wouldn't be lied to and betrayed again? How was I to know if the new leaders were better than the old ones? I was sixteen years old and had lost all confidence.

Democracy, with its endless discussions, its painstaking compromises, was nothing more than party wrangling to me. Out of the question. The whole Federal Republic seemed shabby and petty to me. The grandiloquent words of the Nazi speakers were still flitting through my head. In vain I looked for magnanimity, heroism, readiness to sacrifice. Instead all I heard about was power and money. Petty spirits, I thought.

In the '50s I might have been inspired, perhaps, by people like Ulrike Meinhof and Gudrun Ensslin. But my disappointment at reality and the unreliability of people was too great. I saw the lazy compromises that were made on every side, and my expectations were still out of touch with reality. At that time I saw only two alternatives, anarchism or indifference. Like most people, I chose the more comfortable alternative. One withdrew into the prosperity-idyll. "Not me" was the catchword of the time, Better Homes was the most-read magazine.

During the '50s I read books by Heinrich Böll and Wolfgang Borchert about their war experiences. They helped dissolve my paralysis, thus enabling me to give up my unrealistic stance. I had finally found the human dimension.

Again I recalled the fear of death I had seen in those three young soldiers. Again I saw the wounded, carried into our school because the hospital beds were filled, many of them moaning, others quite still and in strangely twisted positions; a stretcher, the lower half empty but the upper half filled by a young person of normal size. These experiences had affected me for a short time. But the seeds of the propagandists sprouted high and grew over such impressions quickly. For fifteen years I had carried these images in me, unconscious, repressed, forgotten. Now they were there again, clear and strong. The unconscious had preserved them faithfully, until the time was ripe. Personal suffering, death and bodily mutilation had been spared me and those close to me. In spite of this the war had molded me for life.

Only now could I come to grips with the experiences of that time. Only now was it clear to me what war really is: dying, destroying, suffering, poverty and misery. Not courage and honor and the fight for a just thing. It became clear to me. There is no justification for war. I had come to understand the treachery of the Nazi propaganda. It was so easy for them to misuse the people.

Now you will ask: "Did you change your life, after these connections became clear to you?" The answer is no. Why not? I do not know. Perhaps from blindness, from laziness — time passed so quickly. But I tried to pass on to you these realizations. I wanted to teach you respect for life, bring you up so that you would never take a weapon in your hands. I have tried to convey to you that conflicts cannot be solved with force in the long run. Did I succeed? I hope so. But is that enough?

Meanwhile you are almost grown up. Today I know that it is not enough. When the world burns can I not save my own children? And the world will burn, if we don't intervene with all our strength in order to prevent it! We must prevent it!

Anxiety for your sake, for the sake of your future, won't leave me in peace. I can no longer stand by and watch while humanity, in an unprecedented technological insanity, threatens to exterminate itself and all life on earth!

I have told you this quite personal story, not because it is special, but because it is so everyday. I was, to a great extent, spared the horrors of the war. In spite of this I am dragging the inheritance of that time with me throughout my entire life. How much harder must it be for all those whom the war affected more strongly! Even today many still cannot talk about it.

Perhaps I, as representative of the many whose childhood occurred in the years of the war, can make you understand why it is so difficult for our generation to express itself. It took a long time before we could promote something publicly and take part in demonstrations. Only when we recognize that we are not powerless today, as we so like to believe, but that every individual counts, that this is no longer the anonymous crowd, as it was before, when we acted out scenes with the Hitler Youth and swastika flags and were inspired by great words, only when we recognize this will we succeed in acting responsibly, like mature citizens. But even then it will cost us an effort to overcome.

I would gladly have left behind for you, as did our predecessors, a prosperously furnished house. I cannot. What you will take over from us is a sick, wasted, exploited planet, whose surface is eaten away by gigantic cities, industrial centers, weapons arsenals and poisonous garbage, crossed by evil-smelling rivers, covered by dying forests, with violence, poverty and hunger in great parts of the world and superabundance and the arrogance of power in the other.

We, the generation of your parents, have through our indifference, through our indolence, contributed to this destruction. In our lifetime all this has happened and we have allowed it to happen. We have also watched the pileup of death-bringing weapons much too long without doing anything about it. We have understood much too late that the price we pay for our life of abundance and our so-called security is too high. We have forgotten that our ability to rule and use nature for our own ends also entails responsibility.

We must finally recognize that traditional patterns of thought fail when dealing with modern technology. Threatening gestures and muscle-flexing have lost their sense. This method of making an impression goes back to the behavior of our ancestors in grey prehistory, when the chiefs waged man-to-man territorial war. Today the chiefs sit in radiation-proof bunkers when it gets serious, and let their populations exterminate each other. They keep score according to megadeaths. And the megadead — that is us.

Therefore we must succeed in setting aside the traditional ideas of protection and security, attack and defense, as long as there is still time, even when humanity has lived with them for thousands of years. Modern weapons technology puts the decision about the existence or nonexistence of all creatures in the hands of a very few people. It forces us to rethink the role of human beings in nature, if we want to survive. We must recognize our limits, even if the technical possibilities reach far beyond, and reintegrate ourselves into the circle of life. Nothing gives people the right to make themselves lords over life, even when they have the ability to do so.

You must not forget what war is. Even when our words of admonition become a burden — and the memories are painful for many of the older ones — we, your parents, are the witnesses that you need. We must not leave you alone! You have been going into the streets for a long time to fight for a world without weapons and violence. Our generation still knows the grief that a machine gun, a tank, phosphorous bombs can bring.

Today when politicians think aloud about the advantages and capabilities for waging a conventional war, a cold shudder runs up my back. As if no one could remember anymore how it was, when a young man had his face shot away or his legs shattered! When people ran blazing through flaming cities, suffocated by the thousands in bunkers!

Weapons kill. They do not protect. I am afraid for you, for your lives and those of your children. Today when you say, "We shall have no children because there is no future for our children," I can understand you. But I want to do my part, so that our earth will be healthy and a life without fear will be possible.

I have written this letter for you, my children, and for all young people, so you may be more wakeful. I still hope it is not too late. I wish that you and your children will have an active life in a clean and peaceful world. I hope that people will learn to live in harmony with one another and with nature, and that the wounds we have made in our earth will heal.